100 Prison
Meditations

Richard Wurmbrand

Marshalls

Other books by Richard Wurmbrand

Answer to Moscow's Bible
Christ on the Jewish Road
If that were Christ, would you give him your blanket?
If Prison Walls Could Speak
In God's Underground
Little Notes That Like Each Other
Reaching Towards the Heights
Sermons in Solitary Confinement
Stronger than Prison Walls
The Underground Saints
The Wurmbrand Letters
Tortured for Christ
Was Marx a Satanist?
Where Christ is Still Tortured

Marshalls Paperbacks
Marshall Morgan & Scott

1 Bath Street, London EC1V 9LB

ISBN 0 551 01015 0

Printed in Great Britain by Cox & Wyman, Reading

Contents

This is the fourteenth title which I have had published since I arrived in the free world.

I had come to the West, after 14 years in Communist prisons, almost unknown, and not at all familiar with the Western reader.

I owe it to Edward England, a man wholeheartedly dedicated to providing the church with food for souls, that my books could appear, spread and be translated in over fifty languages.

God rewarded his work. The publishing of these books which tell of the struggle, the heroism and the faith of Christians under unspeakable oppression, led to the founding of the International Christian Mission to the Communist World.

Edward England provided the English-speaking Commonwealth with books extolling Christ; this mission in whose foundation he played a decisive role now does the same thing secretly in Communist countries.

Our mission and I express herewith our thanks.

Richard Wurmbrand

Preface

While in Australia recently, I received the news that my daughter-in-law in California had been gravely injured in an automobile accident that demolished the car. Her nine-year-old daughter, who was with her at the time, had also been hurt. When I called California to learn the details, my granddaughter, in answer to my inquiries, exclaimed, 'I have good news! I received a cat for a present!' Then followed a graphic description of — the cat.

Jesus taught us to become like little children, to take a detached view of events, even tragic ones. We may bleed, we may be traumatized, but still we can experience joy in little things that might be considered childlike or unsophisticated.

This is exactly what happened to me in jail.

I spent fourteen years in Communist prisons (not many by Communist standards: the Russian Baptist pastor Hrapov has been in jail for twenty-seven years; the Catholic Paulaitis for thirty-four; the Orthodox monk Michael Ershov for forty-four). We were hungry, beaten, tortured. For years we were individually isolated in solitary cells, where we heard nothing, not even a whisper.

We had no books or writing materials, much less a Bible. We never saw a child, and seldom a woman. We saw no colors: our world was gray. The walls were gray, our uniforms were gray, even our faces were an ashen gray. We soon forgot that blue, green, red, violet exist.

During those long gray months, those leaden years, what did we think about? Certainly not about Communism or about having to suffer. Our minds were too childlike to be controlled by events.

Shakespeare, in *Henry IV*, wrote, 'Thought is the slave of life.' Humanistic philosophy also claims that material conditions determine how our minds work. This might well be true for adults, but not for children. A child lying in a hospital bed after a major accident can have uppermost in his mind a promised toy. We had the same experience. We thought often about things completely unrelated to the pains endured. This is not to deny that everything in jail could be a problem. Will there be many worms in our soup today? Will it contain at least five beans, or perhaps a few more? Will we be allowed to use the toilet? Will I be beaten today? How should I mislead my interrogator so as not to denounce others and cause their arrest? Will I ever be freed? We had problems, but would not allow these to obsess us.

Not long ago, during a board meeting of the Christian Mission to the Communist World, my granddaughter sat on the carpet near us playing with her toys. Overhearing our melancholy discussion of mission problems, she asked, 'O papa, what is "problem"? Where is the word "problem" found in the Bible?' I replied, 'Nowhere.' Puzzled, she queried, 'Then why do you, pastors, worry about something that is not in the Bible?'

This happened years after my release from prison. While in jail, we did not live with problems. Let them beat, starve, mock us. With such things our torturers busied themselves. We were free to rejoice in the mysteries of the Word of God. With such things we kept busy.

I thought about God and about the Bible, about its words, its letters, even the blank spaces between the letters. At times I saw these shapes more vividly than the black letters. During those years the only author I considered apart from the Bible was Shakespeare.

Charles Dickens once said his father gave him this advice: 'Each day read a page of the Bible to know God and a page from Shakespeare to know men.' Perhaps

8

because I am Jewish, and thus basically Oriental, I think much in images, not in propositions. With me in my cell were the Bible characters of old, as well as the saints of all ages — that 'cloud of witnesses' mentioned by Paul. I also saw, as in a theatre, Shakespeare's characters.

From childhood I have possessed a fantastic memory, which, with much exercise, expanded even more in prison (though there were temporary breakdowns as a result of being doped). All prisoners indulged in images. Drugs, which were put in our food for brainwashing, enriched the imagery. But we knew that beyond the images lay the Truth, so complex that even a multitude of images could not exhaust it. We must be able to look at it in its nakedness, in its simplicity. This I attempted to do.

The day I was baptized, the Jewish Christian pastor Isaac Feinstein gave me a verse: 'Reuben [my Hebrew name] shall live and not die.' In a similar vein, Shakespeare said about King Richard II, 'God for his Richard has a glorious angel. Then, if angels fight, weak men must fall.'

With this in mind, I did not waste time, between beatings and tortures, thinking about how badly I had been beaten or fearing that I would be beaten again. Instead, I recited verses of Scripture, Shakespeare, and other poetry. I even composed poems.

'All places that the eye of heaven visits are to a wise man ports and happy havens' (*Richard II*). This even includes Communist prison cells. Atheists believe they put me in jail. I believe God sent me there, to allow me to delve more deeply into the truths concealed within His words.

The outward circumstances, the complete silence, the situation of not being distracted by either sight or sound — all were highly favorable to deep thought. This is when I composed the essence of the meditations presented in this book.

After three years of solitary confinement, we were moved to common cells. There I met with many theologians, some of them exquisite Hebraists or scholars in Greek. Now my thoughts could be chiseled and honed. Later, when free, I could complete the work with scholarly research.

God says we should serve Him not only with all our heart, but also with all our mind. This means intellectual work, hard work. As children we used our brains to learn algebra and geometry. As adults we explore the mysteries of molecules and atoms. When man split the atom, he created the ultimate weapon. Why should we not ponder diligently every atom of the Word of God, however challenging the task, so that we might counter with the ultimate Truth? This desire is strong within me, as I contemplate the words of life that can conquer the destructive forces of godless thinking.

Imprisoned Christians mocked gnawing sorrow. In chains, sometimes in straitjackets and gagged (we were considered mad), awaiting the spectre of death as often as the cell door was opened, we thought about God's Word.

Christians in the free world also contemplate His Word. But because thoughts given by God in those extreme circumstances might resound with a deeper harmony, I publish them. 'They breathe truth that breathe their words in pain.' I am confident that these reflections conceived in silence and nurtured in pain will enable you to delve more profoundly into truth, in order to know *the* Truth.

Richard Wurmbrand

1: The mystery of Jesus' sacrifice

Suppose you were living 2,000 years ago in Palestine, that you were sinful, heavy with guilt, and Jesus told you, 'Your sin is grave and deserves punishment. "The wages of sin are death." But tomorrow I will be flogged and crowned with a crown of thorns for you — I invite you to assist them when they drive nails into my hands and feet and fix me to a cross. I will cry in anguish, and I will share the sorrow of my holy mother whose heart will be pierced by compasssion for me as if by a sword. You should be there to hear my cries. And when I have died, you shall know that your sins are forgiven forever, that I was your substitute, your scapegoat. This is how a man gets saved. Will you accept my suffering for your offenses, or do you prefer to bear the punishment yourself?' What would you have answered?

I believe that this dilemma should be placed before a soul seeking salvation. Fifteen hundred years before the historical birth of Christ the Bible says, 'This day have I begotten thee' (Psalm 2:7). It also says to the penitent 2,000 years after Golgotha, 'Today I die for you.' Jesus' life and death are outside of time and space.

Would you accept? More than once in Communist prisons I have seen a pastor receive a beating to the blood in place of another prisoner. A name would be called and the pastor would simply say, 'It is I.' In Ausschitz, Maximilian Kolbe, a priest, offered to take the place of a Pole sentenced to death by the Nazis. The Pole was the father of many children. The commandant of the camp accepted the substitution and the Pole was spared. Kolbe died by asphyxiation. Had you been that Pole, what would you have decided?

I lived many years in an isolated subterranean prison cell, in timelessness, something akin to the weightlessness experienced by astronauts. Just as they know no difference between heavy and light, I knew no distinction between past, present and future. In my prison cell Jesus' presence was immediate. His life did not belong to the past, nor was it a series of successive events. He put before me the problem which I have put to my readers. He told me, 'You are a sinner and are condemned to eternal punishment for your transgressions, but I am ready to save you. Because of your sin, I will endure rejection, flogging, being spat upon, being crowned with a crown of thorns, the pains of crucifixion and the agony of seeing my holy mother broken-hearted at the foot of the cross. My blood will cleanse you from all sin.' I had to decide whether or not to accept the sacrifice of the innocent Son of God for my sins. I believed that to accept would be a greater wickedness than all I might ever have done in my life and I flatly refused this proposal. Jesus was glad of my 'No.'

Then came the real question, the thing he had had in mind from the beginning. 'What if I incorporate your being into mine, if you become part of my body, if you deny yourself as an independent self, and I will live in you henceforth and you will be "crucified with me" (Galatians 2:20), "buried with me" (Romans 6:4), and share the fellowship of my suffering? People in churches will sing, "safe in the arms of Jesus," while you will be safe as an arm of Jesus, nailed like his to a cross, but also imparting goodness like his. Do you wish to become my co-worker for the salvation of mankind, alleviating sufferings, filling up "that which is behind of the afflictions of Christ" (Colossians 1:24), and imparting eternal life to others? By virtue of my presence in you, the real fruits of my wounds will appear in your soul.'

I have accepted this proposal. Christians are meant to

have the same vocation as their King, that of cross-bearers. It is this conscience of a high calling and of partnership with Jesus which brings gladness in tribulation, which makes Christians enter prisons for their faith with the joy of a bridegroom entering the bridal room.

When George Vins, the general secretary of the Baptist Union of USSR, was sentenced for his faith, believers present in the courtroom covered him with flowers, and his little daughter, hoisted on a stool, recited in front of the Communist judges, 'Father, with Christ you are free in prison, and freedom without Him is prison.' The believers waiting outside the building received him with a Christian hymn.

The relative of a Christian prisoner in Red China said to someone who sympathized with her, 'You should not feel sorry for us, for if he were not in that slave labor camp, how could the others here come to know the Gospel of the Lord Jesus?'

In the same spirit we should receive the crosses of poverty, racial discrimination, personal betrayals, unfaithfulness of marriage partners, rebellion of children and all other sorrows of life.

A man who smugly accepts Christ's dying for him and shouts Hallelujah about the innocent Son of God receiving punishment he himself deserves should be more severely punished than before. The Gospel, the good news, is the privilege of becoming a member of the Body of Christ, of suffering, of dying in pain with Him, and also of being resurrected with Him in glory.

Because sacrifice is implicit in a conversion, the call of the Evangelist has the name 'altar-call.' Every being placed upon the altar in Jerusalem, lambs, rams, and pigeons, died. Someone dies for you. This time it is not an animal, but the Son of God. He has decreed it and nothing you can do will change his mind. You can only ask for the privilege of being able to sacrifice yourself as well henceforth for the glory of God and for the good of

13

your fellowmen. In return you receive the right to die to sin and to the world and its laws.

The reality of a conversion is in becoming one with Him. It is shameful and abominable to accept his substitutionary death otherwise.

2: Why all the suffering?

Reading the Bible in a solitary cell, from memory, I am struck by the extent to which suffering pervades it. It begins with the catastrophy of mankind's expulsion from paradise, and it concludes with the majority of mankind entering hell.

Why do even saints have to suffer? Why are there sufferings in the animal and vegetable kingdoms? Why is a baby born with suffering? Is suffering God's only educational method? Why does evil exist? Why have Christians suffered for decades in Communist jails?

After dedicating 40 years of his life to missionary work among the Australian aborigines, a pastor fell sick. He suffered greatly as he was being transported on primitive roads to the city and was barely able to breathe. He asked his family to sing and to read to him from the Bible. Finally he said, 'Stop praises. I have served Him my whole life and He does not care for me.' He took the Bible from his wife's hand and threw it into the bush. He could find no answer to the problem of suffering.

The only answer which I believe should be given is not to ask the question. Jesus, when He was on the Cross, asked God why he had forsaken even his only begotten Son. His question is followed only by a question mark. All that is revealed to us is that the question exists and that we can live with it.

A sufferer once came to a pastor and asked him many questions. The pastor answered, 'Kneel here in church and ask Jesus for the answers.' The man replied, 'Do you really think I will hear a voice from heaven?' 'No,' said the pastor, 'but by keeping quiet in prayer for several hours before God, you will realize that you can go along without answers to all your problems. This would have been Jesus' answer and it will quieten you.' You do not need more than His peace, which passes all understanding. You do not need both peace and understanding, for understanding presupposes qualifications which most of us do not have.

The Talmud (Haghiga) says that there were four men who ascended to the highest firmament, Ben Azai, Ben Zoma, Elisha ben Abuya and Rabbi Akiva. Ben Azai saw the glory of God and died. Ben Zoma saw and went mad. Elisha ben Abuya became irreligious. Only Rabbi Akiva returned unharmed.

Paul writes about a man who was caught up into paradise, but he could not communicate to anyone about what he experienced because the words he heard in paradise were unspeakable words (II Corinthians 12:2–4).

A legend says that Moses once sat near a well in meditation. A wayfarer stopped to drink from the well and when he did so his purse fell from his girdle into the sand. The man departed. Shortly afterwards another man passed near the well, saw the purse and picked it up. Later a third man stopped to assuage his thirst and went to sleep in the shadow of the well. Meanwhile, the first man had discovered that his purse was missing and assuming that he must have lost it at the well, returned, awoke the sleeper who of course knew nothing and demanded his money back. An argument followed, and irate, the first man slayed the latter. Whereupon Moses said to God, 'You see, therefore men do not believe in you. There is too much evil and injustice in the world. Why should the first man have lost his purse and then become a murderer? Why should the second have gotten a purse full of gold without having worked for it? The third was completely innocent. Why was he slain?'

God answered, 'For once and only once, I will give you an explanation. I cannot do it at every step. The first man was a thief's son. The purse contained money stolen by his father from the father of the second, who, finding the purse, only found what was due him. The third was a murderer whose crime had never been revealed and who received from the first the punishment he deserved. In the future believe that there is sense and righteousness in what transpires even when you do not understand.'

Faith in God is the sole answer to the mystery of evil.

3: Respect poverty

In prison, I come to the lowest level of poverty. I possess nothing, which makes me look in a new light at this verse — 'Rob not the poor, because he is poor. Neither oppress the afflicted in the gate' (Proverbs 22:22).

Do not rob the poor of his only wealth, that precious jewel, poverty itself. St Francis of Assisi spoke about 'sorella poverta,' sister poverty. Ascetics and saints of all ages have abandoned earthly joys for this valuable friend. Moses preferred the poor life of a pastor to being grandson of Pharaoh. Buddha left his father's palaces to know the serenity which only utter poverty can give. Christ, possessor of heaven, chose birth in a stable, life as a carpenter among oppressed people and death among thieves on a cross. He said, 'Blessed be ye, poor, for yours is the kingdom of God' (Luke 6:20).

With what right do I take away the source of a man's blessedness? If I deprive him of poverty, I deprive him of the Kingdom of heaven. Imagine how it would have been had the rich man of the parable (Luke 16:19–31) been what is usually called good-hearted and divided with poor Lazarus his purple robes and fine linen, and invited him to dine sumptuously with him every day. He would have called Lazarus into future hell.

Poverty is the entryway to the kingdom of heaven. The ugly embryonic stage when we look like frogs and apes is the prologue to manhood. Destroy a caterpillar because it is a repugnant worm and you will have destroyed the future butterfly. Taking away a man's poverty, we take from him the source of eternal happiness.

But must we not help the poor? We surely must — by sharing his poverty, by demonstrating our regard for his high estate. Mother Theresa of Calcutta set an example. By sharing the experience of poverty a poor man is given the sense of his dignity before God and other men, whereas a few pennies thrown to him degrade him.

We commonly confound the unpleasant with the bad. Poverty is unpleasant, but it is a Christian's trial of love. What girl is not seduced into admiring a handsome boy who offers her rings and bracelets and cars and castles? Would she choose to live with that same young man in a humble cottage? It was easy for Job to love God with his family and cattle and gold secure. But what was the nature of this love? A trial had to be made in order to strengthen Job's faith.

Before I went to prison, my own social and material situation was very comfortable. In moments of self-examination, I asked myself whether I really loved God or loved rather the many outward and inner gifts with which He had endowed me. Then, in solitary confinement, hungry, trembling for cold, without even shoes — then I could really check whether I loved God or His gifts. How I rejoiced to discover that songs of praise flew from my lips under those circumstances! The faith had been tried.

Christians do not fear hunger and would not readily rob the poor man of this experience. For Jesus says even to the rich, who are familiar with black caviar and other dainties, 'I have meat to eat that ye know not of' (John 4:32). The angel Raphael said to Tobit in the apocryphal book of this name (12:19), 'It seemed, truly, as if I ate and drank with you. But I used an invisible meat and a beverage which men cannot see.' The meat of the angels, of which men also can partake, consists in seeing God, in loving Him even in times of affliction, and in doing His will in all things. You cannot sit luxuriously in restaurants, listening to jazz-music, served by half-naked waitresses, and eating from an endless menu, and at the same time participate at the heavenly banquet. Nobody can have both worlds. Heavenly food is reserved for those who are hungry.

Kierkegaard spoke truly when he said, 'To represent a man who by preaching Christianity has attained and enjoyed in the greatest measure all possible worldly goods and enjoyments, to represent him as a witness to the truth is as ridiculous as to talk about a maiden who is surrounded by her numerous troop of children' (*Attack against Christendom*).

After years of preaching, a pastor should be poorer than before he began his ministry.

Our God is that of the narrow gate and of the needle's eye. If, because of your social position you are not among the hungry, this is a simple matter to remedy: you can fast. But do not rob the poor of poverty. Do not rob the hungry of heavenly manna. Your well-intentioned acts of philanthropy can be robberies.

4: Right attitude toward poverty

It is our greed, our idolatry of money, which makes us equate poverty and unhappiness. The correct attitude of a well-to-do Christian towards a poor one is not pity, but rather envy or emulation. Although you might have more bread than your poor brother, and butter and anchovies upon your bread, 'man shall not live by bread alone, but by every word of God' (Luke 4:4). The poor man has a privilege which you do not: Jesus has been sent to preach the Gospel to the poor (Luke 4:18); only a poor man can fully hear the message. Rich men hear only a watered-down Gospel delivered by pastors who have never hungered or fasted, who are rich or would like to be so.

Such pastors do not wish to lose their rich contributors and preach to them from the Gospel only so much as will not give offense. They never tell their rich parishioners that they have as much chance to enter the Kingdom of Heaven as a camel to enter through a needle's eye, in other words, that their whole religion is in vain.

I repeat the question put in the former meditation: should we not help the poor? Surely we should, but on one condition: not to rob him of his precious poverty.

The way to help the poor is to follow Jesus' example and become poor like them.

We read in the Hebrew book, *Shemen ha tov*, how Rabbi Havyim Auerbach of Launtzitz was once petitioned by a shoemaker who had no wood to heat the room in which his wife and newborn infant lay. The rabbi immediately awakened a wealthy neighbor. The rich man invited the rabbi to come in, but the rabbi said he preferred to speak outside. It was bitter cold and the rich man had to stand shivering on the street and talk with the rabbi for a long time. At last the rabbi mentioned the shoemaker's plight and said, 'Now that you

have felt the cold yourself, you will know what to do.'
The rich man brought wood to the shoemaker's family,
dragging it there himself in a wheelbarrow. Whoever has
not felt the noose about his own neck cannot know the
situation of someone who is in deadly danger.

No welfare state or philanthropic millionaire can replace the charitable works done long ago by monks and
nuns who had taken vows of poverty. These people,
some of them former members of the upper class, gathered the poor into the first hospitals, homes for aged
people and orphanages. They descended in reality and
in spirit to the level of those whom they strove to help,
and truly loved their neighbors as themselves. Embrac-
ing poverty for themselves, they could appreciate its
value for others. The aged, the cripples and the poor
were helped not only with bread, but also by being
brought to regard as a privilege what they had until then
seen as a handicap.

In the United States and other countries there are now
so many poverty programs which do not work. St Francis
of Assisi's program worked. He became poor and influenced many rich men to give away their money, not in
heavily-born taxation, but in jubilating love.

There are diverse manners of giving help. I read that
natives of Portuguese colonies, when they were sick,
passed by the state hospitals and travelled many miles
further to a Christian hospital. When asked why, since
the state hospitals were as well equipped and gave the
same treatment as the Christian ones, the natives answered: 'Yes, the treatment is the same, but the hands
are not the same.' It is only the empty hand that can
caress.

'Neither oppress the afflicted in the gate' (Proverbs
22:22). 'Jesus also, that He might sanctify the people
with his own blood, suffered without the gate' (Hebrews
13:12). Jesus longed to arrive at Golgotha to fulfill the
salvation of mankind. But in those days everyone, even
executioners with victims, were stopped at the gates to
answer questions, to show their papers. I too have seen

it. It is not easy to be taken outside a prison gate, not even for an execution. The executioner knocks at the gate: the guard looks suspiciously through the peep-hole, then checks the written order. So it was also in times before.

It is written in Proverbs, 'Do not oppress the afflicted in the gates.' Those who belong to Jesus are so happy to bear afflictions for His sake: do not stop them again at the gates to question them, to slow down their heroic march towards self-sacrifice by offering them pardons or conditions. By doing this you further oppress the afflicted ones who glory in their afflictions for Christ's sake.

A Christian must so conduct himself that his children will joyfully say like Jacob, 'God of my father' (Genesis 32:10). Jacob had ancestors of whom he could boast. Abraham had left the highly civilized Ur of Chaldee, living as a stranger in a barren land in order to be free to worship God as he knew best. Isaac was ready as a child to magnify God by his death. Such men should not be robbed of the afflictions which promise them an eternal weight of glory.

Affliction has its difficulties. Often you are overcome by despair. God seems to have hidden His face from you. But then you realize that it has only been for sport, like play with a child. You seek Him, find Him again, God and you, both exhilarated, both open wide with joy.

There is a deep teaching in the Talmud: 'Before a man eats and drinks, he has two hearts.' He feels both his own hunger and another's. Once he has eaten and drunk, he remains with only one heart, with thought only for his own comfort.

Instead of robbing the poor of poverty and the afflicted of the affliction which will constitute his future glory, see that you yourself are among the men with two hearts.

5: Untruthfulness in Biblical personalities

We cannot tell the Communist interrogators the straight truth about our church activity. If we were to give frank replies to all their questions, more arrests would follow. We remember Rebecca used an immoral ruse to give Jacob the blessing normally due to Esau as first-born (Genesis 27). The ethical value of an action is judged not only by its accordance with certain moral rules, but also by its long-range results.

If Rebecca had not done this, Isaac would have given the blessing to Esau. Then Esau's descendants would have been the chosen people instead of the Jews. Some savage would have had to try to become the Savior of the world. Wild men would have been the holy prophets.

What catastrophy if Rebecca and Jacob had not cheated and lied in that one circumstance! Their behavior was part of God's plan. Isaac's sight had grown weak so that Jacob might be mistaken for Esau and receive the blessing.

Obviously to take such action even in exceptional circumstances is a dangerous choice. Others will justify their selfish deceits by holding up what you have done for holy motives as an example.

The Midrash says: 'Jacob later married Rachel, but on the marriage night, Laban, her father, substituted Leah, a girl whom Jacob disliked (Genesis 29:23–25). In the morning, he saw he had been cheated and told Leah, 'During the night, I called you so often, "Rachel," and you answered. Why did you deceive me?' She said, 'Your father called you "Esau" and you pretended to be your brother. You deceived your father. No teacher is without a disciple. I have learned from you.'

We must be aware of this danger but Christians cannot altogether forego the serpent's wisdom.

Can a Christian be a police inspector, an undercover agent, a diplomat or an officer in war without using ruses?

How could the underground church survive in countries where there is persecution if it did not follow Rebecca's example? Such strategies are shocking because they are the exception to the Christian rule of complete truthfulness.

Words are spoken for various purposes other than for communicating truth. Sometimes they serve self-defense, like the words of Paul, 'I have committed nothing against the people or the customs of our fathers' (Acts 28:17). In I Thessalonians 2:14–16, Paul had burst out against the Jews, and he had also done more than trespass against certain customs. He had nullified an essential part of Jewish law when he declared circumcision of no value. But now he was in danger of death. In such cases, in moments of crisis, words have to be the servants of another master than truth.

Old Testament Joseph said, 'I was stolen away out of the land of the Hebrews' (Genesis 40:15). This was not the fact, but we can appreciate his desire to cover up the sin of his brothers who had sold him as slave.

Let us have in view the many sides of human life when we judge the ethics both of Biblical personalities and of our fellow men.

6: What is Caesar's?

Many Christians have submitted to Hitlers, Stalins, Maos and the multitude of lesser white, black and yellow dictators. Many did it with good intentions, guided by the Lord's words, 'Render unto Caesar the things which are Caesar's' (Matthew 22:21).

The words have been misunderstood. Jesus did not advise his disciples to give anything to Caesar. His words were addressed to the Pharisees. Has an order given to a German soldier any validity for a British soldier? The Pharisees and Jesus' disciples were at odds with one another: the words were spoken to Jesus' detractors, not to His friends.

Jesus had no coin of his own — 'They brought unto him a penny' (v. 19). Jesus' foes were caught in Caesar's monetary system, while Jesus' disciples owned nothing.

The Hebrew Bible does not even contain the verb 'to have.' Christians consider possession to be wrong, for they are only administrators of God's possessions. Owning nothing, the Christian could owe nothing to Caesar.

Who was this Caesar anyway? A foreign conqueror who had occupied Palestine, he had contributed nothing to its well-being. He had never planted a tree, built a highway, or even visited the country. Yet he had established tax-collectors to milk its riches, and had slaughtered anyone who dared resist his edicts. Nothing in Palestine belonged to Caesar.

If you say to a Czech, Hungarian or Pole, 'Render to the Soviets the things which belong to them', he would understand you instantly. Nothing belongs to them. These words can only mean, 'Give them a boot in the back and send them packing.'

This was also the sense of Jesus' words. If the Pharisees were so convinced that they served God, why were their minds preoccupied with things which are not godly? Jesus commands them, 'Do both things: serve a tyranny and serve God at the same time.' He knew they would soon realize that these things are not compatible. One must choose between being Caesar's bootlicker and a true servant of God who stands before a godless king liked Herod and tells him to his face, 'What you do is unlawful.' This is the attitude which cost John the Baptist his head.

It is a misuse of Jesus' words to interpret them as counseling submissiveness to despots. My own interpretation is in fact the contrary. Just as the soul is higher than the body, so the sacerdotal dignitary excels and instructs the regal; the celestial, the terrestrial. It is the duty of kings to obey church leaders, rather than the reverse.

7: Someone missing in Jesus' genealogy

'Who can believe in the Bible's inerrancy?' a pastor once asked me. 'I can show you at least one sentence which is positively untrue. It is Matthew 1:17 where we find the assertion that there were 42 generations from Abraham to Christ. But there are more in the genealogy of Luke 3 and in those of the Old Testament.'

There is an even stranger aspect to Matthew's genealogy. Matthew was a publican and he knew how to count accurately. He claims to give the names of 42 generations. But if you thoroughly check, you will find that he only gives 41 names.

It is not immediately apparent that one person is missing. Attention to verses 11 and 12 of Matthew 1 reveals that one and the same Jechonias is counted twice. The genealogy is divided into three groups of ancestors, each of 14 persons, but the last person of the second group is also the first person of the third group.

There is one name wanting in this list: it is yours. Jesus has to be conceived in you as utterly as he was conceived in the womb of virgin Mary.

Jesus said, 'Whosoever shall do the will of my Father

which is in heaven, the same is my brother, and sister. . .' Up to this point His words are easily comprehended. Every believer can be His little brother or sister. But He offers one other possibility; He says, '. . . and mother' (Matthew 12:50). We can be mothers to Him, insofar as Jesus is conceived in us. His relationship with us will encompass that of son and mother, and we will be motherly towards Him.

All love contains an element of self-interest. You love father — he gives pocket money; you love mother — she gives candies. Your brothers and sisters are also your playmates. Only motherly love is completely unselfish. I know of a mother beaten to death with an axe by her son who, before she died, asked him whether he had hurt himself in doing it. A mother's love exists without asking any return.

Your attitude toward Jesus can be motherly. Then you will be the 42nd generation, the missing link in his genealogy.

Matthew's text was not meant to be simple history; nor was it meant to give mathematically precise figures, but rather figures which have a symbolic meaning. Both Matthew and Luke give a multiple of seven as the number of Jesus' ancestors, 42 in the first case, 77 in the other. Seven in the Bible is the holy figure, a topic which will be explored in a later meditation.

One could say it is untrue that a coronation confers a kingdom, but it is a true symbol of its being conferred. So in the same way, the generations from Abraham to Jesus were not truly 42. Matthew himself gives only 41 names. But the report contains a true spiritual message.

Something can be true without being factual.

8: Male and female words

For many years I never saw a girl or a woman. This increased my curiosity regarding everything to do with the feminine.

Like most languages, Hebrew has male and female nouns. English, which has the same article for all nouns, is an exception in the family of human languages. In German, 'table' is male and has the article *der*, 'lamp' is female and has the article *die*, 'bread' is neuter and has the article *das*. Adjectives and verbs also take different forms according to the gender of the noun. This is also true in Slavic and Latin languages.

The Hebrew has not only male and female nouns, but also male and female forms for one and the same noun. For example, 'ship' is *ani* in its male and *anijah* in its female form. *Shir* and *shirah* are male and female forms of the word 'song.' *Erets* and *Artsah* are the two forms for 'earth,' *asham* and *ashmah* for 'sacrifice.'

The male and female forms represent the active or passive aspects of the nouns in question, and their usage can greatly affect the inner meanings of many passages in the Bible.

Even when he writes in Greek, a language in which the noun does not have this peculiarity, John considers 'the great winepress of the wrath of God' (Revelation 14:9) as not being so cruel a thing as it would seem. According to the rules of Greek grammar, he has to use the masculine gender for the noun, 'winepress,' but he defies the grammar and puts the adjective 'great' in the feminine gender to show that with God even wrath has a gentle character.

The suffix 'ah' in Hebrew usually indicates feminity. Women's names often end with 'ah,' as in Bathshebah, Dalilah or Sarah. However this ending also shows direction in the sense of 'tending toward.' What is thus expressed in the genius of the Hebrew language is that objects tend toward a female, passive or subject form. They all begin by asserting their independence, but in the end will all be submitted to the will of God.

Ruah, the Hebrew word for spirit, is female. In Genesis 1:2, 'And the spirit of God moved upon the face of the waters,' the verb 'moved' also takes the feminine form. Thus an exact translation of these words, a rendering which would reproduce a Hebrew's feeling reading them would be: 'The female spirit moved in a womanly manner upon the face of the waters.'

The frequent name for God in the Hebrew Bible, 'Adonai Sabaoth,' means not just 'the Lords of hosts,' but, exactly translated, 'the Lord of the female hosts,' like, 'the Amazons.' Male and female Christians both, all who believe, are *brides* of Christ and warriors with feminine characteristics. The direction for all of us must be toward acquiring more female characteristics: gentleness, quietness, submission, passive acceptance of everything the Bridegroom decides.

Biologists have discovered that all fetuses are created female. Later the Y chromosome sends a flood of male hormones over some fetuses, causing them to develop into males. The Y chromosome does this work by producing H-Y antigen, a substance found in the cell walls of all men, but not in women.

Every embryo is female in the beginning. Through becoming brides of Christ, through putting ourselves in the feminine position toward Him, we return to our original state, to the purpose for which we have been created, to be Christ's brides.

A male, at conversion, also becomes a bride of Christ, not a bridegroom.

9: Manner of breathing

New prisoners ask us, 'How can I resist torture?' Among many other pieces of advice, we tell them, 'Breathe deeply, rythmically.'

Paul writes, 'Whatsoever ye do, do all to the glory of God' (I Corinthians 10:31). This includes a saintly manner of breathing.

Life of mankind began when God breathed the breath of life into Adam (Genesis 2:7). In what rhythm and manner will God have breathed?

The Bible speaks about many kinds of breathing. The sinner is compared to 'a wild ass that snuffs the wind at her pleasure' (Jeremiah 2:24). Jeremiah also speaks about men who neigh after their neighbors' wives (Jeremiah 5:8). The persecutor Saul of Tarsus is described as 'breathing out threatenings and slaughter against the disciples of the Lord' (Acts 9:1). Jesus Himself had a breath apart. 'He breathed on His apostles,' and they received the Holy Ghost (John 20:22). Orthodox priests still breathe on persons as part of the baptismal rite.

What is your manner of breathing? Do you exhale anger, lust? Or do you have the quiet, majestic, serene breathing of a man who has no attachment or repulsion toward the world, and who is undisturbed by it? Such breathing must be practiced.

Yoga exercises can be useful but do not solve problems. A man can practice yoga in the morning and begin to neigh and to breathe hatred in the afternoon. One must practice breathing to the glory of God in the moments of greatest temptation. When others shout at you or torment you physically, when you are in danger, or are attracted toward sin, proceed slowly and begin to breathe in the holy manner: deeply, evenly, rhythmically. This will help you be a victor.

The language of the Bible teaches us to be attentive

to our manner of breathing. In Hebrew, *Ketsar af*, 'short of breath,' is the expression for 'impatient'; *ereh apaim*, 'long of breathing,' means 'patient, serene.' The states of our souls are connected with our breathing. When one breathes deeply for ten minutes in a slow, even rhythm, consciously thinking, 'Now I inhale; now I exhale,' anger becomes impossible. One who has the foolish desire to become angry can practice breathing in the opposite manner.

Do everything to the glory of God: even the manner in which you breathe is known by the Almighty. Trees breathe slowly and live long; insects, the contrary.

10: Unintelligible words

The Bible contains in its original, words whose meaning we do not know, e.g., *Eshpar* in II Samuel 6:19 and I Chronicles 16:3. The Authorised version translates it 'flesh,' but puts the word in italics to show that the meaning is uncertain. Some Jewish commentators translate it as 'cake of dates.'

No one is sure of the meaning of the words *Selah* and *Miktam* which are frequently found in the Psalms. The renowned Jewish interpreter Rashi says that *selah* means 'eternally.' Ybn Ezra thinks it is a musical sign. The Septuaginta translates *selah* as 'pause.'

Miktam appears in the heading of Psalms 16, 56, 57, 58, 59 and 60. The Midrash, a Jewish commentary, says David was humble (*makh*) and righteous (*tam*), hence, *miktam*. Rashi believes it is, like *selah*, the indication of a melody. Ybn Ezra and Luther derive the word from *Ketem* — 'gold.' A note in the Authorized version calls

Psalm 16 'a golden Psalm.' Others consider the Babylonian word *kafamu* as the source of *miktam* and translate, 'a psalm of atonement.' All of these are guesses.

The Greek word *epiussion*, which appears in The Lord's Prayer (Matthew 6:11), exists nowhere else in Greek literature. The English translation 'daily' in the expression 'daily bread,' is arbitrary. Jerome used 'our supersubstantial bread.'

There are many other words whose meaning remains in mystery. One possibility is that no meaning at all should be attributed to such words. Nowhere does the Bible affirm that everything in it must have meaning.

The '*Mumonkan*,' a 12th Century fundamental book of Zen Buddhism, says, no-meaning is the meaning of the walkers of the 'way.'

The Hebrew text of the Bible has musical notations. The Old Testament is a song in which some sounds are there simply for their musical beauty, without any sense, like the 'Tra-la-la' in popular songs of modern nations.

The whole Bible is an inimitable symphony. Not only the meaning of the sentences, but their very sound can move the soul to ecstasy. To give just one example: in English we read that the multitude of believers were 'of one heart of one soul' (Acts 4:32). This is a deep thought, but in Greek it is beautiful sound also, a rhyme: 'Kar*dia* kai psyche *mia*.' Letters, syllables, and whole words could have been written in the Bible just for the splendor of the sound. Anyone whose ear is attuned will enjoy them. They cannot be translated.

Luther called our reason 'a beast' because of its tendency to interfere in religious matters. The rational mind seeks sense and logic in everything, including the Bible. But why should the Bible be bound to make always sense to the mind? It speaks rather to the soul.

Krüger, the president of the Boer republic, went hunting, leaving behind his sick wife with a sick child. Upon his return he heard his wife singing, which was not her habit. Entering the house he found her sitting in bed with the dead child in her arms. Within a short time she also died, still clinging to the baby.

Forsaking everything, Krüger tramped through fields and forests, trying to make sense of life and love, which unite us for a time, until death forcibly separates us. His friends, alarmed, sought him for many days and found him hungry, singing and with deep peace in his heart. He had not found the meaning of things, but he had given up seeking.

Why must we always apply logic and syllogism to everything? Why not simply sing a melody, as the nightingale does, without constructing meaningful sentences? It is in its music that the deep sense of the Bible is to be found — where the heart simply sings, sometimes in unintelligible words, about the unintelligible ways of God.

Thinking like this, I did not mind when my speech became blurred, because of the circumstances in which I was detained.

11: Almah

Everyone would consider it bad taste to publicly discuss or write about whether his wife was a virgin at marriage, but many debate whether Mary was really a virgin when she gave birth to Jesus.

In many circles it is contested whether Isaiah really prophesied the virgin birth. The argument is that in his words (7:14), 'The Lord Himself shall give you a sign: Behold, a virgin shall conceive,' the Hebrew expression 'almah' does not necessarily mean 'virgin.' It could also mean 'young maid.'

Like other nouns in Hebrew, the word 'virgin' has two forms. *Elem*, the male form is always used for a very young boy who could not have known woman yet, like David when he killed Goliath (I Sam. 17:56). In this passage the authorized version translated *elem* as 'stripling.' The word occurs again in I Samuel 20:35 in reference to 'a little lad' who accompanied Jonathan.

Since *elem* in the male form surely indicates a virginal boy, why then should the female form, *almah*, not also have the inference? Surely Matthew the Evangelist knew better Hebrew than the modern professors of theology, and his translation of Isaiah's prophecy was, 'a *virgin* shall be with child' (1:23). For myself, I would believe in the virgin birth of Jesus even if it were not written in the Bible.

We humans all have split characters. How could it be otherwise, since we inherit from our parents features which come from two divergent and often contradictory lines? Jesus, however, was One: He is not ravaged by inner antagonisms. His heritage comes from a single line.

You can rely on the Bible. Mary was a virgin when she conceived Jesus. The One who kept her pure and holy by His grace will also see that you appear before Him with virginal purity.

12: The double sense of the word 'netzah'

They gave me twenty-five years, which was practically the same as life imprisonment. The day I received the sentence, the followings thoughts occurred to me. Hebrew Biblical words have a cluster of meanings, giving them a spectrum like that of the rainbow. Let us examine two meanings of the word *netzah*. This word can mean 'perpetual' — 'Why is my pain perpetual?' asks Jeremiah (15:18). But *netzah* also means 'victory' (I Chronicles 29:11 and Isaiah 25:8). Thus, what appears to be a despairing, unanswered question in Jeremiah could also be faithfully and literally translated, 'Why is my pain? It is to serve victory.'

It is said that King Solomon once stood at the seashore admiring the fleets of many nations passing by. He asked the high priest who was standing beside him, 'How many ships a year to you think pass through our waters?' the priest answered, 'Only three.' The king, thinking the priest was being insolent, said indignantly, 'How dare you give such a reply? I see dozens of ships at this very moment.' — 'An illusion,' responded the high priest. 'In reality all ships sailing on all the seas are only three: the ship of desire for money, that of desire for fame, and that of desire for pleasure. These are the three forces which drive through the seas, whatever name a vessel takes for a while.'

The king pondered this for some time. In his Song he had foretold of a fourth ship, a very small one, unable to navigate beyond the small lake of Galilee, but in the end surpassing all others. This would be the ship of the Messiah, a ship powered by the sacrifice of the Son of God, by intense love, by the desire to serve.

It sails in defiance of all the laws of hydrodynamics. The wonder accomplished by the Messiah when the tempest ceased and the ship was rescued at his command is an even greater miracle than is commonly thought. Mark wrote that the waves had beaten into the ship, 'so that it was now full' (Mark 4:37). Any vessel thus full of water will sink whether the sea is stormy or calm. But this ship, the ship of Jesus, does not sink, not even when the waters of sins, crimes, schisms, heresies and persecutions have filled it to the brim. It advances toward victory.

Its 'perpetual' (*netzah*) great sorrows are but the shadow of the *netzah*, the victory toward which it sails.

13: Two senses of 'sabahtani'

'*Eloi, Eloi, lama sabahtani*,' was Jesus' cry from the Cross. The Evangelist translated these words from the Aramaean: 'My God, my God, why hast Thou forsaken me?' But this is not the only possible translation.

Sabahtani is the first person, past tense of *Leshabeah* which means 'to forsake.' But *leshabeah* also means 'to glorify.' It is frequently used in this sense even in modern Hebrew prayers. So the words of Jesus could have been translated, 'My God, my God, to what (degree) have you glorified me!' These were the words with which the Therapeuts, a subdivision of the Essenian sect of Jesus' time, finished their prayers. It was an expression of amazement at the multitude of graces received.

On the last evening, the Lord prayed, 'Glorify thy Son' (John 17:1), probably using the Aramaean word, *meshabeah*. The apparent result was not glorification, but being abandoned by most of His disciples, being flogged, mocked, crucified, and forsaken by God. Is this how the heavenly Father answers prayer?

But Jesus' supplication that evening could also have had an entirely other, mysterious, sense: 'The hour has come. Our plan should now be fulfilled. Forsake, reject (*shabeah*) thy Son, that thy Son may glorify (also *shabeah*) Thee through bearing everything with patience and love.' Thus the whole Passion which followed is a consummation of Jesus' prayer.

It may also seem strange that Jesus' words, 'You have forsaken me,' are in the past tense, while He was being forsaken then and there — the crucifixion was a very present event. Why then does Jesus use the past tense? Ordinarily someone would not ask while being beaten,

'Why *did* you mistreat me?' He would say, 'Why *do* you beat me?' using the present tense.

One of the secrets of spiritual strength is to live outside of time. A present day revolution with all its immediate horrors is difficult to endure. But we can easily bear reading about the French Revolution and its guillotine of 200 years ago. God and the spirit live eternally. Eternity is not timelessness, but life beyond time. You can decide how you wish to regard an episode of your life, in the present or in the past. Everyone sometimes evokes pleasant memories of the past and relives them as if they were present. The opposite can be done as well. You can transfer today's difficulties into the past, thereby enabling yourself to cope with them serenely. In this manner they cannot break you. This is how we resisted.

14: How to examine yourself

Solitary confinement tempts you to endless brooding over your past life. St Paul writes, 'Let a man examine himself' (I Corinthians 11:28). How should one proceed? There is no specific instruction in the Bible, but Christian experience of hundreds of years has taught us at least one thing: Do not be too thorough in self-examination. A little creature in the laboratory can be examined so extensively that it dies from over-exposure.

Rather than examining all the details of your own life, try to fathom the depth of your faith in the value of Jesus' life, death and resurrection.

Once a man was greatly concerned about the state of his soul. No sermon or religious book could satisfy him. Finally, he heard about a hermit who was reputed to have great wisdom. The man took a horse and rode to the mountain top where the sage lived. He found the sage in meditation at the entrance to his cave. The sage asked the man what he desired. 'I seek salvation,' said the man. The sage was silent for a long time. Then he said, 'Why don't you seek a horse instead?' — 'I have a horse,' the man replied. Turning toward the rear of the cave, the sage remarked, 'So that is it,' and said no more.

As the man rode down the mountain on his horse, he thought and thought about his meeting with the sage. All at once he was enlightened: Why should he seek a horse? He had one. He was riding on it. Therefore why should he seek salvation: God sent His Son into the world that the world might be saved through Him. Salvation was already assured. A man riding on a horse should not bother to seek a horse unless he had overtired or killed the one he has. The Savior can not be exhausted. Unless a man flees from salvation, unless he consciously refuses it, he has it without much ado. Jesus has come to seek and to save what is lost. We do not have to seek Him. His desire for us to be in paradise is much greater than our own. His desire to forgive our sins is much greater than our desire to be forgiven. Salvation cannot be sought, but only accepted. When the man arrived in the valley, he understood.

Christians often say, 'I was saved five or fifteen years ago.' This can not be so. We were all saved 2,000 years ago, when Jesus died for us on Golgotha. Perhaps it was only five or fifteen years ago that we realized it.

When we approach Holy Communion, the main thing we must ask ourselves is, 'When I hear the words, "This is my blood, shed for you for the remission of your sins," do I understand them as clearly addressed to me? Do I know as surely as a rider knows he has a horse under him, that my sins are forgiven and forgotten and dealt with?' If I understand this, I have examined myself well and am worthy of Holy Communion.

15: The Bible's imprecise time

I lost the notion of time, I didn't know what hour or what day it was, my solitary cell being subterranean, I didn't even know if it was spring or summer.

The authors of the Bible knew their lives are eternal. Time did not matter for them and so they were quite imprecise in dating events.

In John 21:1 we read, *meta tauta* — 'after these things Jesus showed himself again.' How long was it 'after these things?' You search in vain.

Chapter 3 of Matthew starts with the words, 'In those days came John the Baptist preaching in the wilderness of Judaea.' In the preceding verse, John and Jesus could not have been more than 2 or 3 years old, so three decades must have elapsed before John began his public ministry. For the Evangelist it was still 'in those days.'

Both John and Matthew are speaking about events between which much time passed, as if they took place simultaneously. Before Einstein this would have been considered inaccurate. Now we know that a statement about the simultaneity of two events acquires meaning only in relation to the place where an observer is situated. It belongs to the subjective part of our observation, not to the objective part which constitutes history.

The spirit blows wherever it wishes, says Scripture (John 3:8). Wind and spirit is the same word in Greek. I can place myself spiritually in a position such that events distant from each other in time appear to occur simultaneously. It is like some Americans who like to watch two or three TV programs at the same time.

Can the preaching of John the Baptist occur 'in those days,' e.g. at the time of his childhood? This is how Matthew saw the events. Who am I to accuse him of inaccuracy?

We have a promise, 'Ask and it shall be given you' (Matthew 7:7). This verse seems to contradict much of our experience. Every believer knows of answered, but also of unanswered prayers. We have asked and were not given. But how much time has passed since we asked?

Moses asked God, 'Let me go over and see the good land that is beyond Jordan.' The Lord answered, 'Let it suffice thee; speak no more unto me of this matter' (Deuteronomy 2:25–26). Here is an instance not of an unanswered prayer, but of a prayer clearly refused. How does this fit with, 'Ask and it shall be given you?' Well, a little later, some 3,500 years, or, to use the Biblical expression, 'in those days,' Jesus was on mount Tabor with his disciples and 'there appeared unto them Moses and Elias' (Matthew 17:3). Mount Tabor is in Canaan, beyond Jordan, in the promised land. So Moses' request was finally granted, only with a few thousand years delay. Not much for one whose life is eternal.

We have before us not an eternal life, but eternal lives. The Hebrew has no singular for life. Most Hebrew nouns which end with 'im' are plural, and the Biblical word for life is 'haiim.' We will have a multitude of lives and opportunities. I believe that all prayers will be answered.

Eternal life is more than infinite. Kantor, a Jewish disciple of Einstein, conceived the notion of 'transfinite.' When you draw an endless line in one direction from a given point, its mathematical value is ∞, infinite. But when you draw from the same point two or more endless lines in different directions, you have something beyond the infinite. Kantor calls it 'the transfinite,' and uses the Hebrew letter *Aleph*, for its mathematical symbol. The possibilities of eternity are inexhaustible. 'Ask and it shall be given you.' Do not ask when. Heaven is outside of time.

Periods of time in general are not objective physical facts, but are dependent upon the observer. Time and space are by their very nature confused representations of the only real thing: the interval in the space-time continuum! Let us think biblically, outside of time.

16: The things beyond the Bible

The Bible contains what God revealed to us, taking into account the condition and capacity of our hearts and minds.

Jesus told His disciples, 'I have yet many things to say to you, but ye cannot bear them now' (John 16:12). We wonder what He would have said, had we been capable of receiving all His words.

The Biblical authors have left many interesting things untold. Paul complains that time fails him 'to tell of Gideon, and of Barak, and of Samson and of Jephthae; of David also and Samuel and of the prophets' (Hebrews 11:32). Much of Paul's time was absorbed by dealing with all the trifling questions which produced so much strife among the first Christians.

Jude had intended to write about the most important subjects of 'common salvation' (Jude vs. 3). We have remained without the knowledge of his thoughts in this matter because he had instead to exhort the believers to beware of 'ungodly men' who had crept into the leadership of the church.

Biblical authors also had to adjust their messages so as not to offend the prejudices of listeners. The first Christian sermon, that delivered by Peter on Pentecost, calls Jesus simply 'a man approved by God' (Acts 2:22), 'exalted by the right hand of God' (Acts 2:83) Peter does not say that Jesus is the Son of God. This would have been too difficult for the Jews to accept. Diplomacy is a factor in all intelligent preaching.

We must come to understand not only what the pastor says, but also what he might have said, had we been open for the whole truth.

When a statue of Krüger, the president of the Boer Republic, was made in Pretoria, Krüger's wife asked the sculptor to make the President's top hat hollow so that when it rained the birds could drink from it. Those familiar with the history of the Boer Republic are inspired by this statue, encouraged to emulate that great statesman in their own actions. Birds get from that same statue only a few drops of water.

If we do not remain little birds in faith, we will come to know what the authors of the Bible could not tell their contemporaries. The river of life, will give us more than a few drops of water.

God passes us through prison to give us new ability to understand.

17: Euphemisms in the Bible

Some tortures are obscene. If ever freed, should one tell what happened?

The Bible consistently avoids mention of an essential part of life, an aspect overworked to the point of offence in current language: The word 'sex' never occurs in the Bible, nor do words for the sexual organs or sexual intercourse. The latter is replaced with 'to know': Adam *knew* Eve his wife' (Genesis 4:4). For the female sex organ, the word commonly used is 'the shame' — *boshet*, or sometimes 'the navel' (Song 7:2). The general tendency of Biblical style is toward euphemisms.

This applies not only to sexual matters. In Acts, we repeatedly find the expression that Jesus was 'hanged on a tree' (Acts 5:30). The crucifixion evoked too gruesome a picture.

Scripture also avoids telling the complete story of certain wrong actions. In Genesis 35:22, in the Authorized version, the word 'it' is written in italics, a type used whenever the translators have added something to the original text. In Hebrew this sentence remains incomplete: 'Reuben lay with his father's concubine. Israel heard.' We would expect to be told the details of the incest and of the terrible clash between father and son, which must have followed. However the Masoretes left a blank space in the Hebrew text after the words, 'Israel heard,' to teach us that the worst in bad things is better left unsaid.

In Genesis 4:8, after the words *Vaiomer Cain*, 'And Cain said,' the Masoretes left another blank space with a circular mark indicating an intentional omission of something important.

Both the Samaritan text of Genesis and the Septuaginta, the first Greek translation, add at this point that Cain said to his brother, 'Let us walk out into the fields.' The Syriac version is, 'Let us go to the desert.' But knowledge of a more far-reaching discussion between the brothers seems to have been kept orally. The Targum, an Aramaic paraphrase of the text, adds that Cain said, 'I thought that the world has been created in mercy, but it is not governed according to merits of good works, nor is there any judgement or a judge, nor shall there be any future state with rewards and punishments. Why is my sacrifice refused?'

The Bible as given by God prefers to pass over Cain's words with silence. By such omissions we are taught not to reproduce or quote the words of wrongdoers. Such words are too often contagious.

The Bible also avoids the use of epithets. The Jewish historian Josephus Flavius of the first century wrote that Pilate was a corrupt and cruel mass-murderer. We know from the Talmud that the high-priests of Jesus' time were merchants more than servants of God, stooges of the Roman empire, who obtained their high positions through bribes. But the Bible gives no reproach against the personal lives of Caiphas and Pilate. It tells only what they did to Jesus. The Evangelists did not consider it their calling to publicly denounce their sins.

We know from historical sources that the lives of the whole Herodian dynasty was debauchery. The Gospels report only the minimum about their dealings with the children in Bethlehem and with the apostles. One private sin is mentioned only because it led to the death of John the Baptist.

We, who delight in every defect which we discover in an adversary, benefit by emulating the Bible's use of euphemisms and silence.

18: A language without the word 'word'

The word of God was given through the Hebrew people. This can be asserted clearly in any language except Hebrew itself. The chosen people, the depository of the word of God, have no specific word for 'word.' They use *davar*, which also means 'thing.'

The Evangelist John wrote in Greek, but thought in Hebrew. In his native tongue, the prologue to his Gospel would read, 'In the beginning was the *Davar*, the thing, and the thing was with God and the *Davar*, the real thing, was God.'

To speak in words which have no substance in reality is to chat, not to speak.

You cannot comprehend the Bible if you look at it as a mere collection of words.

The Mamunkan, one of the great books of Zen Buddhism (13th century) says, as if animated by the Hebrew spirit: 'Words do not express things; phrases don't show the mind-movement. He who receives only words is lost; to stagnate with sentences is to be deluded.'

It is obvious that words can express only words, not feelings, experiences or objects. The latter express themselves without words.

As Einstein has connected space with time and has created the concept of the four dimensional space-time continuum, the Hebrews conceived the unique notion of '*davar*' the thing — word with two aspects, one verbal and the other in the physical or spiritual reality.

In Hebrew Jesus could not have said simply, 'Thy word is truth' (John 17:17). He must have used here *davar*, which is more than 'word.' Words alone, even divine words are not the truth: they can be cloaks for cruelty, strife and greed as well as inspirations for holiness. 'Thy *davar*, thy word-thing, in its double aspect, is the truth,' just as, after Einstein, events are no longer placed only in space or only in time. Instead we have the notion of 'interval' in physics, which comprehends them both.

The Italian sculptor Tommassi ornamented the cemetery of Buenos Aires with statues, each representing one of Beethoven's symphonies. When a friend asked me to describe them, I found myself at a loss for words.

Beethoven expressed what he felt in notes which, when played, give sounds. The sculptor carved in marble what he felt when he heard the music. I looked upon the figures of stone. If I put my own feelings into words, what relation would they bear to Beethoven's symphonies?

A blind man once asked a friend to describe milk to him. His friend began, 'Milk is white.' The blind man stopped him with a second question, 'What does white mean?' — 'White is the color of a swan,' was the reply. The blind man then asked, 'What is a swan?' The explanation was, 'It is a bird with a bent neck.' He persisted in questioning. 'What does "bent" mean?' The friend bent his elbow and said, 'Touch my arm now and you will understand what I mean by the word "bent".'

The blind man touched his friend's elbow and exclaimed, 'Now I know what milk is like!'

If the Bible is only an accumulation of words, we will know about God only as much as the blind man knew about milk.

We have to arrive through the words to the real thing, to God Himself. Only then will we be illuminated.

A man asked a saint, 'Who is God?' The saint replied, 'Who are you?' The man said, 'I am so-and-so.' The saint asked, 'Do you know so-and-so?' He said, 'Of course.' The saint held up a dust-whisk and asked, 'Do you see the dust-whisk?' the man replied, 'I see it.' The saint stopped the dialogue as useless.

'God' is a sound produced by English-speaking people to communicate about a mysterious being. Another, a small mysterious being, myself, about whom I also know almost nothing is called 'Richard' in English. French people pronounce the name, 'Rishaar,' and Germans in a manner which cannot even be approximated in English spelling. I see an object which the English call 'dust-whisk.' It is used for wiping dust away only by adults. Children would regard it as a toy. It can also be useful for spanking or for drawing a line.

With men who remain in the sphere of words, discussions lead nowhere. Words are useful only if they lead out of the realm of mere chatting to the '*davar*', to the reality-word.

With what words could I explain God? Should I say He is a King? This is a title which many good men, but also Herod, Nero and Henry VIII bore. I might confuse minds calling Him 'King.'

Should I call Him 'Father?' Luther had a very harsh father and was reluctant to address God with the words of the Lord's prayer.

Even 'God' is a word used not only for the Creator, but also for cruel beings like Moloh and Quetzlcoatl who asked thousands of human sacrifices.

We have to pass from simple words to the *davar*, the

real thing, in order to apprehend God, not only Creator, but also Keeper and Destroyer.

19: Don't trouble Him

Just as death was an unspeakable pain for Jesus, His birth must also have caused Him great anguish. It is written in Acts 10:44, 'The Holy Ghost fell' The advent of the Spirit, which for us in uplifting, is for Him a fall. 'The seeds fell,' says Jesus in the parable of the sower (Matthew 13:4). Before developing into wheat, they must first fall from the hand of the Master. Later Jesus explains that the seeds stand for different types and qualities of men (Luke 8:12–15). For each one, the coming to earth is a falling. This is the meaning of birth for every man. How much more must the birth of the Son of God have been a descent, the pain of which He preferred not to mention. The depth of His fall is shown in the fact that He is put in the most humble place, a manger.

We Christians are so bold as to sing, 'Come into my heart.' But what sorrows await Him there! Many faithful souls, foreseeing how their faults will grieve the Master, repeat Peter's words as he fell down at Jesus' knees, 'Depart from me, for I am a sinful man, O Lord' (Luke 5:8).

The Roman centurion, instead of inviting Jesus as we do, told Him, 'Lord, trouble not thyself: for I am not worthy that thou shouldst enter under my roof.' This officer was praised for his faith above all others in Israel. What a contrast to our habit of troubling Him about all manner of trifles, and never being willing to appeal to an angel. We insist on summoning the Master Himself for our needs and ask whenever possible for visible signs.

A really loving soul is careful not to disturb the Beloved. I know about a girl who was in love with a young man whom she knew to have a great career ahead of him. She felt that, being uncultured herself, she would be a burden for him in society. He loved her heartily, but she refused his advances and caused him to marry another girl, more suitable for his social status. Sometimes the greatest love is shown in renouncing the beloved.

Jesus' coming to earth was a great agony for Him. His coming to fulfill your prayer troubles Him. So many were healed of blindness simply by asking, and then, with eyes wide open for the world's temptations, they ran after their lusts, forgetting to Whom they owed their sight. Christians must renounce many things. Renounce also your many requests. Give Him peace in the hours when He wishes to be alone.

Should you not trouble Him even when you are terribly hurt? Perhaps not, for what will you do should Christ accept your prayer and alleviate your suffering? Might this not mean a terrible loss for you?

Once, in his sleep, a man swallowed a venomous snake which stuck in his throat. He awoke in terrible pain, but not knowing its cause. A woodsman, a man of experience, passing by, fiercely beat the man until he was black and blue. At last the snake was vomited out and slithered away. Had the man begged the woodsman to give him peace, and had his request been granted, he would have died.

None of us receives more blows than absolutely needed: 'the very hairs of your head are all numbered' (Matthew 10:30). Our lives are foreordained. Does our heavenly Friend not also know how many sufferings we must endure?

Do not trouble the Master. He knows.

20: Exaggerations in the Bible

Much has been written by believers about the Bible's accuracy, but its obvious exaggerations are seldom mentioned.

'To Jesus of Nazareth give all the prophets witness,' says Peter (Acts 10:43). But there were Hebrew prophets like Obadiah or Amos who did not ever mention the Messiah.

A Samaritan woman who met Jesus told people, 'Come, see a man which told me all things I ever did' (John 4:29). This certainly cannot be accurate. It would take years to reveal someone's every action. Jesus had shown her only that he knew of her many sexual transgressions.

Critics would say that such statements are inaccuracies which entitle one to call the Bible into doubt. But those who know the human heart learn from such statements about the impact Jesus made upon his contemporaries.

During World War II, my wife went to Budapest under dangerous circumstances to bring relief to the suffering Christians there. For a long time we had no news from her. During that time, I was unable to read anything without seeing her picture on the pages of every book or newspaper I opened. I could have said like Peter, contrary to the experience of other men, 'All books and magazines contain only Sabine's image.'

For a time after her interview with Jesus, the Samaritan woman was obsessed with the remembrance of all her mistakes, and in such a state of conscience she could truthfully say, 'He told me all things I ever did.'

For Peter, who had seen the risen Lord and was full of the experience of the Messiah, it must have seemed that all the prophets had spoken only about Christ. It was just while Peter was speaking in this way, which normally would be considered exaggeration, that 'the Holy Ghost fell on them.'

Many Christian preachers and writers are too insistent on accuracy. The Holy Ghost does not fall on those who listen to them because Jesus is not their all. They are filled with observations and thoughts about other things besides the Lord.

The apostle Paul also exaggerates when he says, 'All they which dwelt in Asia heard the word of the Lord Jesus' (Acts 19:10). But Paul never went farther than Asia Minor. Persia, Russian Asia and China were unknown to him. Paul 's assertion shows with what his mind was consumed: not with wealth, fame or pleasure, but with a dream so strongly felt that it seemed real: Asia at the feet of Jesus.

Such dreams are truth. A simple description of facts is uninspired boredom. God's truth has wings; it sees the distant future as being present.

I could well understand Paul's assertion when, after my liberation, I was preaching in Taiwan. Although I was speaking before only 10,000 persons on a small island of China, this was not how I experienced it. Before my spirit and before my eyes were the 900 million of mainland China who have no way to hear the Gospel. It was to them that I spoke.

Every night during my years in solitary confinement, I delivered a sermon to my congregation at home. I was sure that my words reached them. Words are heard not only by those whose physical ears perceive the sound. Perhaps Paul knew more about telepathic communication than we do.

It is an exaggeration to consider something as exaggeration simply because it appears so to us. It is not that the Bible exaggerates; we exaggerate in criticizing it.

Many things which previously were considered Biblical exaggerations have later proved true. Moses called Palestine 'a land that flows with milk and honey,' an obvious boast (Deuteronomy 26:9). But recently a scien-

tist has shown the earth to be capable of over three times
its present food yield, and cited Israel as an example:

(1) The average cow in Israel produces 50% more of
milk a year, compared with the U.S. average.

(2) In Israel, an orange grove is yielding 16 tons of
fruit a year — a world's record.

(3) An acre of peanuts in Israel grows twice as many
as are grown on Jimmy Carter's peanut farm.

(4) Cabbages and tomatoes grown in Israel are among
the finest anywhere.

All of this is achieved despite limited rainfall in this little
country. So Moses' boast is not such an exaggeration
after all.

Biblical authors regard numbers as unimportant. On
the day of Pentecost, when the Christians of Jerusalem,
120 of them, were gathered together and became filled
with the Holy Ghost, Peter explained the occurrence as
being the fulfillment of a prophecy of Joel: 'It shall come
to pass in the last days, says God, I will pour out my
Spirit upon all flesh' (Acts 2:17). A hundred persons can
hardly be called 'all flesh.'

Such statements are normally called exaggerations.
But if a man cannot readily find simple words for his
feelings, if he clothes them in superlatives, should we
call this a lie? Is *Faust* a lie because Goethe, feeling the
power and complexity of evil, personified it as Mephi-
stopheles? Peter was so overwhelmed by the fiery cloven
tongues which had sat upon each of the disciples (Acts
2:3) that he could not speak except in superlatives.

Nehemiah exaggerates too when he says, 'Thous hast
multiplied the children of Abraham as the stars of heav-
en' (9:23). But there are billions of stars, not that many
Jews.

The Bible is an Oriental book. One cannot appreciate
its truth by applying Anglo-Saxon standards to it. The
rules of truthfulness vary from one culture to another.
In the Anglo-Saxon world, a statement is true only when
it exactly fits reality. In fact, understatements are often
preferred. With the Japanese it is otherwise. It is correct

to say what is pleasing to your interlocutor, even if this
is not the real state of affairs. Hyperbole is the normal
for an Oriental. God has made His revelation to us
through an Oriental book, and the Bible is inerrant
according to the Oriental mentality which produced it.

21: Sayings missing in the New Testament

It is important to observe in the Bible not only what it
contains, but also what is omitted.

One of the interesting features of the New Testament
is that Jesus never asks anyone to tell Him about the
circumstances of his sins. He knew men to be sinful, so
the details of their trespasses, be they small offenses or
huge crimes, did not interest Him. Instead of probing
in dirt, He went from one man to another saying, 'Be of
good cheer, son; be of good cheer, daughter. Your sins
are forgiven.'

Another important feature is that no one ever says to
Jesus, 'Please, forgive me,' or 'I am sorry.' On the last
evening all the apostles fled and one denied Him. Later,
when the resurrected Lord appeared to them, it would
have been seemly for them to ask His forgiveness. None
did.

Whoever looked into Jesus' face saw there so much
love and goodness that he felt, 'With Jesus forgiveness
is self-evident. His willingness to forgive me is much
greater than my readiness to ask for forgiveness. His
wish for me to be saved is far greater than my own. His
desire for my fellowship in heaven is greater than my

wish to go there.' We do not have to approach Jesus with words of apology, but only trusting in His goodness.

There is something else that cannot be found in the New Testament: Jesus never turned down anyone's invitation. To refuse an invitation would be foreign to His nature. You just invite Him into your home and heart. He accepted invitations even from His worst enemies. He will surely accept yours.

Let us be attentive to the verses missing in the Bible.

22: Words missing in the Bible

Now that, being a prisoner, I have nothing, I realize the importance of the fact that in the Old Testament the verb 'to have' never occurs. It does not exist in the Hebrew language, not even in modern Hebrew. To lack even a word for expressing the idea of having is real 'not having.'

It is sinful to have. All the first Christians who were 'possessors of lands or houses sold them and brought the prices of the things that were sold, and laid them down at the apostle's feet' (Acts 4:34–35), They were Jews and discovered, thanks to Jesus, what had long since been revealed through the genius of their language: it is wrong for God's people to have. A child of God can only administrate things which really belong to the Creator.

In Greek the word *echo* is used for 'to have,' but it has several other meanings as well: 'to be able,' 'to be possessed with,' 'to can,' 'to count,' 'to do,' etc.

The idea of 'having' is a false notion. I was born

without my consent — I did not choose the time or place, my bodily shape or my inherited character. My life developed in circumstances which were largely not of my own forming. I do not 'have' my life. It proceeds according to laws established beyond myself. Nor do I have the things appertaining to life.

The renowned tenor Caruso was obliged to sing in the opera on the day of his mother's death, in order not to disappoint the thousands of fans who had come especially to hear him. After the performance he exclaimed, 'I believed in the beginning that I had a voice; now I realize the voice has me.'

Even joys and sorrows are given or withheld by others, and in the last analysis, by one other Being.

Not only is the infinitive 'to have' absent from the Hebrew vocabulary, but even the genitive case is little in use. In Hebrew one does not normally say, 'the house of a man' because nobody is meant to own one. In everyday Hebrew speech the genitive is replaced by the so-called 'construct case,' which consists in shortening the word for the thing possessed. Thus any person or object which is reduced to the position of being a possession loses value.

In the Lord's prayer the word 'I' is missing completely, although it is one of the most frequently spoken words in the prayers of men.

There is one thing worse than praying before an idol: praying before one's own image and bowing to it.

Christians should not be I-centered, but God-centered. The 'I' should completely disappear in prayer, even as a reminder of the identity of the person who prays. True prayer is an outstreaming of love so pure that all that matters is the good of the whole and the will of God.

Another word which is completely absent from the Bible is the word 'history.' History is the record of events as they succeed each other in time. In history an event is assumed to be the effect of preceding events which are its cause. All this is illusion. What I see in a cinema also seems to be a succession of events, but the projectionist could have run the film backwards, showing the events in inverse sequence, or the film could have been spliced to put the events in a different order. Everything is pre-determined by God. The pen with which God has written all things which will happen until the end of the world has long since dried, and will not again be dipped in ink to write an alternative version.

23: Interesting biographies missing in the Bible

The New Testament recounts repeatedly and in great detail the life history and conversion of the persecutor Saul of Tarsus to Paul the future apostle, although there must have been other biographies which at the time, when Acts of the Apostles was written, seemed more interesting than that of the persecutor.

Paul said, 'Many of the saints did I shut up in prison . . . and when they were put to death, I gave my voice against them. And I punished them oft in every synagogue and compelled them to blaspheme' (Acts 26:10–11). Not only had he killed Christians, he broke their resistance and made some of them become apostates.

These were the first renegades and martyrs of Christianity, but the Bible does not report their names or even tell the story of their suffering, betrayal or heroic death.

Perhaps the Biblical authors wished to prevent future abuses in the veneration of saints. In later centuries, stories of martyrs were told in minute detail and often embellished with fantasy.

The Bible says about the fellow-prisoners of Old Testament Joseph, who was put in charge of them, 'Whatsoever they did there, he was the doer of it' (Genesis 39:22). Likewise Christ is the doer of the lives of martyrs. It would not have been Biblical to make a great fuss over them; they themselves would not have desired it.

Why should martyrs be so honored? What they have done is not the maximum, but the minimum required from a disciple of Christ. Even to be like Christ in life and death would be below what could be expected of him. Whoever is *like* Christ is not Christ. We are meant to *be* Christ. We are the body of Christ — so we are He. 'You will be *like* God,' the devil said to Eve. 'Ye are gods,' said Jesus. The union between the believer and God is perfect. Martyrdom is a small thing in comparison with this calling.

Other highly interesting biographies are absent from the Bible. We are told in Acts 2:41 that on one day, in Jerusalem alone, three thousand souls were added to the Church. Did they remain steadfast? Did they, in their turn, bring others to the Church?

Why do you need answers? We continually hear about many who accept Christ at evangelical mass rallies. What happens with these people afterwards? Are their decisions sincere?

Whoever puts many questions gets many depressing answers. The Bible teaches us to rejoice that some men had at least partial good will and good intentions, even if only for one day.

A Samaritan woman brought her whole town to Christ (John 4:30). Had she continued like this, no unconverted cities would have remained in Palestine. The Bible tells us only what she did on that one day. After this a veil is thrown upon her life.

A thief, Zacchaeus, promised under the Lord's influence, to give half his goods to the poor and to restore fourfold what he had stolen (Luke 19:8). The Bible story concludes with his promise, but we are not told whether he fulfilled his pledge. The holy author rejoiced that a thief showed even a single moment of contrition.

Jesus praises an officer as being the most faithful man he had ever met (Matthew 8:10). It would seem to be instructive to know how this officer continued his life. A man who is faithful today might not always remain so. However the Bible does not give us whole biographies, but teaches us to rejoice in the little and transitory good we find in men.

24: Echad and Iachid

An ancient Chinese parable tells of a hunter who went out to set traps with his son. The son, despite all warnings, set the traps on the road, instead of waiting to arrive in the forest. Soon many people were caught in the traps, including the boy's mother and sister. Next love and truth and hope were caught, and finally even the road fell into the snare. The world remained without a road.

After a long time, the father convinced his son to unlock the traps. The road was so happy to be free that it stretched out until the whole world became a road. 'How beautiful *my* road is now!' exclaimed the boy. The road, hearing that someone claimed it as his possession, died. Since that time there has been no road in the world.

It is a pessimistic story. There *is* a road to God. The Bible is His revelation, a map that must be read with careful attention to its wording. This road also cannot be claimed by anyone as 'mine': it is God's only.

The Bible's main teaching is that God is one; our faith and baptism are one. But the Hebrew language has two expressions for the concept 'one.'

Iachid stand for absolute oneness, as in Genesis 22:2:

'Take thine only son Isaac, whom thou lovest. . .' *Echad* represents composed oneness as in Genesis 1:5: 'It was evening and it was morning, one day' (so in Hebrew).

God is never called *iachid* in the Hebrew Bible, but always *echad*, a composed unity. The literal translation of Deuteronomy 6:4, the keystone of the Jewish faith is: 'Listen, Israel, Jehovah, your gods (plural) is a Jehovah of composed unity (*echad*).'

'God was never alone, but, being the only One, was many, for He was not wordless, nor wisdomless, nor powerless, nor counselless' (Hippolyt). 'There are always present to Him the Word and Wisdom, the Son and the Spirit through whom and in whom He made all things freely and spontaneously' (Irenaeus).

God knows Himself with perfection. This self-knowledge is called the Eternal Son. He possesses all the attributes of the Father whom He knows. The two are united in perfect Divine love. This love also has all the attributes of the Father. We call this love Holy Spirit. The three entities are one. This oneness is *echad*, composed, a oneness between entities who also retain their distinction.

The 'Zohar,' an ancient book of Jewish mysticism, referring to Deuteronomy 6:4, also proclaims God as a Trinity. Asking why God's name appears three times in this verse, it answers: 'The first, the Lord "Jehovah," is the Father above. The second name is of Jesse, the Messiah who is to come from the family of Jesse through David, and the third is the way which is below, and the three are one.'

The atom, nature, the individual — all are unities. Parts in a state of extreme tension achieve the miracle of oneness.

There is oneness in diversity, and tension even within the Godhead. 'It pleased the Father to bruise His son' (Isaiah 53:10). The Son, in agony in Gethsemane, begged the Father to spare him. The Father's decision stood.

Jesus said, 'Who has seen me, has seen the Father'

(John 14:9). In this also true when you have seen Jesus weeping and in despair?

Jesus also spoke the mysterious words, 'If I go not away, the Comforter will not come unto you' (John 16:7), giving the impression that the two cannot be in the same place at once.

We commonly say that Jesus is our mediator and intercessor with the Father, which seems to imply that the son intervenes to change the Father's decision in our favor.

God is one, *echad*, not *iachid*. If His Unity were not so complex, there would not be such a great need to proclaim it.

The Church is one, man and wife are one — *echad*, composed unities. Believe in Oneness despite diversity and tensions which sometimes impair the basic harmony. This Oneness cannot be broken.

The way is not your property. Nobody can possess the One. The one God, the one Church owns us.

25: The mystery of unanswered prayer

The Bible is full of unaccepted prayers.

Paul writes, 'Without ceasing . . . I make request . . . to have a prosperous journey by the will of God to come unto you' (Romans 1:10). Instead of a prosperous journey, he traveled as a prisoner in fetters and was shipwrecked. Other examples abound throughout the Bible.

Every request in prayer shows a lack of submission to what God in His wisdom and love has foreordained.

What would the world be like if God were to change his plan every time someone expressed a desire in prayer?

The Talmud says that the Jewish high-priest entered the most sacred place of the temple once a year to pray for the people, and always concluded his prayer with the words, 'God, disregard the requests of Wayfarers.' This was wise: everyone who travelled on Monday asked that there be no rain on that day; likewise those who travelled on Tuesday, Wednesday, etc. If God listened to them all, the people would perish because of drought.

The following story illustrates the best manner of prayer. Two Christians each planted an apple tree in front of his house. When the time for reaping apples came, the first looked angrily at his tree: it bore not even one apple. When he approached his neighbor's house, he became even angrier. The branches of his brother's tree were cracking under the weight of beautiful fruits. He asked his brother, 'Explain this to me. We planted our trees at the same time; we serve the same God. How is it that He gave you so many apples and none to me?' The other answered, 'Perhaps you did not pray for your tree.' 'What! Not pray?' said the first, 'I prayed every day: "God, give rain; God, enough, now stop the rain. God, sun is needed now; too much now, it might scorch my tree." I never neglected prayer, and it was all in vain. How did you do it?' The brother replied, 'I am not so keen at prayer as you are. I prayed only once, in the beginning, like this, "Father, I have planted an apple tree and wish to have fruit in due time. It is not for me to teach you how much sun and rain to give. You are a more ancient gardener than myself. You created Eden and all trees grow under your direction. Grant me apples in due time." '.

We experience unanswered prayer because we ask for too many things without knowledge of their long-range results. There is really only one Christian request: 'Here I stand, a sinner forgiven by grace and, at the end of my life, I pray to dwell in heaven with my beloved ones.

Teach me to serve You on earth as I journey toward your heaven.' Such a prayer never goes unheeded.

26: Why did Jesus choose a devil as apostle?

Under Communist pressure, some pastors became renegades. Does this annul the value of their messages of times before?

'Jesus said: One of you is a devil. He spoke of Judas Iscariot' (John 6:70–71). If Jesus knew Judas was a devil, why did he choose him to be an apostle?

We learn the word of God from the psalms of David, a murderer and adulterer, who normally should have spent his life in prison; from Solomon, never satiated with women and in the end an idolater; from Peter who turned coward when courage was required. God chose these men to teach us to distinguish between the message and the sins of the messengers, to accept our teachers in spite of their weaknesses and their great sins. If we were to reject works of art produced by immoral men, there would remain almost no great works of art.

We are all strengthened by the hymns: 'There is a fountain filled with blood drawn from Immanuel's veins,' and 'God moves in a mysterious way his wonders to perform.' These and other familiar evangelical songs were composed by William Cowper, who later became a national poet of Britain, but never again used his gift in the service of God.

Cowper wrote in his hymn that sinners plunged beneath the blood of Christ lose all their guilty stains. But about himself he wrote, 'There is no encouragement in the Scripture so comprehensive as to include my case, nor any consolation so effectual as to reach it.' He admitted the free forgiveness of God's love to every case except his own: 'I believe myself the only instance of a man to whom God will promise everything and perform nothing.'

Does this tragic change of attitude, which Cowper kept until his death, diminish his value as a hymnist? We have to distinguish between the song and the composer.

In the West, the lives of political leaders, high ranking officials and even Church leaders are probed with such thoroughness that even the archangels would not be found faultless if submitted to such examination. We might better simply ask, 'Does this man perform his political, economical and religious duties well?' The rest belongs to God. No one is without sin and even men who have committed grave offenses have been useful in the kingdom of God.

Perhaps it was to teach us this that Jesus went to the extreme of appointing a devil as an apostle. He could not have chosen worse than that.

27: Why did Jesus not allow himself to be made a king?

When Jesus perceived that the Jews would make him a king, he departed (John 6:15). Surely he would have been a better king than Herod and He must have known it. Why, then, did he not accept?

We can only postulate his motives.

One reason would be that the choice would not be His. Nations are fickle: today they elect a king; tomorrow they overthrow him. Christ does not accept the roles we choose for Him. The choices must be His. His decision was to be a Savior for eternal life rather than a king in this life.

On the other hand, the fact that He was a good Savior does not prove that he would have been a good king over Judaea, just as a good Sunday school teacher might not necessarily be a good prime-minister.

As man, He sometimes showed utter indifference toward human suffering, just as he could also show compassion. None of these attitudes dominated him.

He chose among them. He was told about innocent Galileans killed by Pilate. A kingly person in the earthly sense would have shown indignation and would have organized the tyrant's overthrow. Jesus said simply: 'Suppose ye that these Galilaeans were sinners about all the Galilaeans, because they suffered such things? I tell you, Nay: but, except ye repent, ye shall all likewise perish' (Luke 13:2–3).

He is told about a catastrophy, a tower which has collapsed killing eighteen people: Jesus does not give instructions about building more safely in the future, nor does he organize relief for families of the victims. He repeats the above words and makes this another occasion for teaching repentance. He acknowledges only one real motive for grief: that of not being a saint.

This is the correct attitude for a Savior, but not for an earthly king.

When Jesus heals a man inhabited by demons, He causes a large herd of swine to drown (Luke 8:33). Jesus shows callousness toward this destruction of property. But it was acceptable for a Savior to destroy a herd and leave someone impoverished in order to heal his fellow man, and therefore Jesus does not justify himself, nor do the evangelists defend his action.

He achieves the objective to be expected from a Savior. For an earthly king such behavior would not be right.

Jesus predicts a national tragedy: the destruction of the Jewish state. He does not call upon men to risk their lives in defense of their fatherland as a secular king would have to do. He tells his disciples, 'At such time flee' (Luke 21:21). The abandonment of their countrymen at such a tragic time forced the final break between Christianity and Judaism.

The Savior had entrusted the disciples with a deposit of eternal truth which had to be kept intact. This was more important than the defense of their land.

So thinks a Savior. An earthly king has another calling. These two purposes do not mix.

Jesus could not be an earthly king, and those who try to make Him the Solver of earthly problems are mistaken.

28: Why the outbursts of rage with Jesus?

The Bible teaches that God is love. It does not teach that He is all love or only love. His actions also have other aspects.

Job said, 'God has delivered me to the ungodly and turned me over into the hands of the wicked. . . He has broken me asunder, he has also taken me by my neck . . . and set me up for his mark. His archers compass me round about' (16:11–13). When I read these lines, I envision St Sebastian pierced with arrows from all sides by the persecutors of Christianity. Job would say that God was the first cause of what Sebastian suffered.

Job surely believed in one God, but speaks as if there were a plurality in Him. He describes God as one would describe an enemy, but says in the same chapter, verse 19, 'My witness is in heaven,' which means he visualizes God as one who takes his defense.

Jesus represented God on earth. Whoever saw Him, saw the Father (John 14:9). Jesus could not be all love.

He sometimes bursts into what seems to be unmotivated rage. The Pharisee who invited him to dinner did not make any unkind remark to Jesus or about him, but merely wondered why Jesus had not washed his hands before the meal. Jesus began to vituperate at all Pharisees, calling them fools and hypocrites.

A lawyer, another guest, tried to do what I also would have done, in an attempt to appease Jesus. In answer, Jesus speaks harshly about all lawyers and even about the lawyers' fathers (Luke 11:38-52).

Anyone would have objected to such behavior from a guest.

It is best that we accept God and Jesus, his messenger, as they are. It is wrong to impose human ethics and human patterns of behavior upon God.

Jesus wished to die crucified, this being the only way to pay the ransom for human sin. In order to be crucified, he had to arouse violent hatred toward himself. Without this hatred, neither the atoning death of Jesus, nor our salvation, could take place.

The first apostles had the same aim, knowing that the blood of martyrs is the seed of the Church. They also willingly evoked hatred towards themselves.

In Rome some Jews believed the message of Paul, others not, but he generalized in accusing the whole nation, 'This people is waxed gross and their ears are dull of hearing' (Acts 28:24-27).

Jesus and his apostles often did things which filled others with anger. It was necessary. Similar behavior is practiced sometimes in the underground church today.

29: About eternity

Eternity is not endless time. Such a thing does not exist, as there are no spaces without dimension. Eternity is a state in which time no longer exists (Revelation 10:6). The philosopher Boethius has given the definition generally accepted by the Christian church. Eternity is 'the total, simultaneous and perfect possession of an endless life.' As the Greek thinker Parmenides put it: eternity is whole, unique. In eternity nothing has been or will be. 'All is at once, one, continuous.'

Imagine a motion picture. When we view it through the projector we see the events recorded on the film successively, and each one seems to be the effect of those preceding. Once in a cinema I found myself praying for an innocent man suffering terribly on the screen. I implored God to save him. But what was to happen was already recorded on the film. My business was only to behold.

We should live with the perspective of eternity in the present, in perfect serenity. Everything has been fore-known, predestined (Romans 8:29). As Omar Khayyam expressed it so well:

'With earth's first clay, they did the last man knead
And then of lhe last harvest sow'd the seed.
Yea, the first morning of creation wrote
What the last dawn of reckoning shall read.'

Islamic tradition attributes to Mohammed the words, 'The pen wherewith God has written all things which will ever happen has long since dried.' Christians, too, believe in predestination.

Therefore the ideal attitude for a believer is the contemplative one. Jesus says, not just to Martha, but to all men: 'Ye are careful and troubled about many things, but one thing is needful, and Mary has chosen that good part' (Luke 10:41–42). Almost every Christian today would say she had made the wrong choice: she had chosen not to prepare a dinner for a dozen hungry men, but quietly to behold the beauty of the guests.

Nowhere does the Bible enjoin us to 'Be active,' but on countless occasions we are told, 'Behold,' behold without interfering. 'Behold, there came wise men' (Matthew 2:1). Instead of beholding them, men showed them the way to Bethlehem, and it cost the lives of many innocents. 'Behold, there came a leper and worshipped Him' (Matthew 8:2). At that time, men knew no cure for leprosy. Do not interfere unless you are sure of being able to help. Just behold; the Lord will do the rest.

'Behold, there arose a great tempest in the sea' (Matthew 8:24). One of two things will happen: either you will drown and go to the Father, or you will escape and live for the Father. So, do not panic but simply behold. In all things, the bigger the fuss, the more discordant the results.

We are not yet in eternity, but we can catch a glimpse of it by passing as much time as possible in quiet contemplation.

30: The quest for God

The quest for God is old.

An Ugarithic poem, 'Ludlul bel nemequi' ('I'll praise the Lord of wisdom') dated 2500 years B.C., contains the moving verse:

'Oh, that I only knew that these things are well pleasing to a god.

What is good in one's sight is evil for a god.

What is bad in one's mind is good for his god.

Who can understand the counsel of the gods in the midst of heaven?

The plan of God is deep waters. Who can comprehend it?'

Men seek the right relationship with God but as his will, his predilections, and thoughts are unknown to us, we tremble at every step that it might sever the loving relationship.

Such fear disappears only when we pass from relationship with God to possession of God.

In Jesus, the Son of God became man. A marriage-feast between the divine and the human natures took place.

I can now say, 'I am my beloved's and my beloved is mine' (Song 6:3). He is my possession. He disposes of me, but I also dispose of Him. It is no longer a relationship between two entitites who can at any moment become separate. The barrier is broken by Christ. God is no longer alone, and the tormented heart of man is no longer single. The heart now responds to God in Shakespeare's words: 'No more can I be servered from your side, than can yourself in two divide' (*Henry VI*).

The difficulty of not understanding God's way disappears. 'Shall the thing formed say to him that formed it, why hast thou made me thus?' (Romans 9:20)? the soul which possesses God knows that His control of the world cannot be judged by man's myopic view. 'The deceived and the deceiver are his' (Job 12:16). He who possesses God is satisfied with this and asks no questions.

On the last day, the Lord will say to some, 'I never knew you' (Matthew 7:23). How can a Creator not know his creation?

He created us, but not as creatures external to Himself; He created us that we might live and move and have our being in him (Acts 17:28). He desired union with us in an eternal embrace and not as a knower/known duality. Those rejected in the end will be those who have not realized this and have remained knowers of God.

They have had a relationship with a distant God, perhaps even a good relationship, prophesying in his name and casting out devils and doing many wonderful works (Matthew 7:22), but they remained separate from God, unpossessed of Him. They did not belong to their beloved, and their Beloved was not theirs.

The renowned Christian mystic, Meister Eckhardt teaches that he who adores God is an unbeliever. Those who believe unite with Him, and no one is left to be adored.

31: Relative weight of wonders

When I wondered why God does not free us through an angel, as it happened when St Peter was in jail, I remembered that in Acts 2, there are 27 verses about the teachings given by apostle Peter and only nine words about miracles: 'many words and signs were made by the apostles.'

Miracles play a minor role in the Christian religion primarily because it is too easy to regard as miraculous what is not.

Missionaries who went to the Ambrim tribe in the New Hebrides preached without success until they took out their artificial teeth and put them back again. This was the start of a breakthrough. The chief exclaimed that the gods had come to them in the likeness of white men.

Many healings considered miraculous have no more value than that, although I myself have also experienced real miracles of reconstituted health.

What takes place after the miracle can also be a problem. In Shakespeare's Henry VI, when the king heard about a blind man wonderfully cured, he said, 'By his sight his sin is multiplied.'

If regeneration does not accompany the cure the former blind man will be possessed by new passions which will make him a worse man than before. This is also true of other infirmities. I have personally known blind persons healed to the great detriment of their souls.

We should also have in view that some of the Biblical miracle stories derive from questionable translations. We are told that Elijah was fed by ravens — orevim — in Hebrew (Kings 17:6). The same Hebrew word is used in Isaiah 15:7 for 'Arabs.' What if Arabs fed the prophet?

There have been so many miracles in the course of history. They do not usually convince anyone except sometimes the person who benefits. Jesus told those who sought him, 'Ye seek me, not because ye saw the miracles, but because ye did eat of the loaves' (John 6:26).

In the search for miracles what counts is the satisfaction of the desires of the self. But Jesus teaches us to deny our selves. If the self is not mortified, every miracle only increases the demand for more and magnifies egoism. So the Bible does not emphasize miracles, but rather the teaching which brings about new birth.

Let us walk securely according to the Biblical teachings, and if God does a miracle, let us rejoice.

32: The crime of fear

It is fear which made some Christians around us become Judas's.

Revelation 21:8 enumerates eight categories of men

who shall have their part in the lake which burns with fire and brimstone. First on the list are not the unbelievers or murderers as would be expected, but the fearful.

Fear is so human. Peter feared in Gethsemane. We all do, but it is more abhorred by God than many gross offences. It seems that there are many battles ahead even in eternal life. God's universe is vast and courage will be one of the great criteria of selection.

A Christian never flies except to the devil's throat. He can say of himself what King Charles of Frances says in Shakespeare's 'Henry VI': 'Him I forgive my death that kills me when he sees me go back one foot or fly. My army, rather with their teeth the walls they'll tear down than forsake the siege.'

We are Jesus' sheep. Sheep do not run from the wolf. They cannot defend themselves, but they witness for their Creator by enduring their deaths patiently, without turning their backs to the enemy.

Children of God can be burned at stake, but they cannot be made to give in. We are assigned to be the scourge of demons.

When Henry VI said, 'Of all base passions, fear is the most accursed,' he expressed a Biblical thought.

33: Science and the Bible

Not only Biblical authors, but also other sages of antiquity knew things which modern science is only now discovering. Aristotle, Greek philosopher of the third century B.C. wrote in 'On the generation of animals' that lead ore increases in size and becomes thick and white when air gets into it. Until the beginning of this century this idea was considered to be just an oddity from barbaric times.

Some 70 years ago, flotation was discovered by the modern world. Powdered mixture of ore and rock is mixed with water and air forced in. The ore becomes white, increases in bulk and floats on the surface of water. This process is used today on millions of tons of ores all over the world. So the ancients knew something after all.

The more so ancients inspired by God, the authors of the Bible: it is foretold that at the return of Jesus 'the Mount of Olives (on which he will stand) shall cleave in the midst thereof . . . and half of the mountain shall remove toward the north and half of it toward the south' (Zecharaiah 14:4). The Quarterly Journal of the Geological Society 1958, tells that the rocks in the Jordan Valley are in considerable tension, that the valley is in a state of shear. This means that geologically, the whole Mideast is moving northwards. Science makes us wait for the moment of the mount's cleavage, but we wait also for His feet to touch its peak. We are not fools.

Science has shown what a big influence genes, climate, food, sickness and bodily structure have upon our characters. The phases of the moon and the spots in the sun are factors in our behavior. The greatest incidences of crime occur during the hottest months of the year.

Our minds are complex, but our souls even more so. Who in antiquity knew about the Oedipus, Electra and Pygmalion complexes, etc., about the innate subconscious which can lead us to commit terrible deeds? Because of these things, some say, the Biblical moral criteria are obsolete.

It is true that many in ancient times were ignorant. But there was One who knew what was in man (John 2:25) and because He knew, He taught, 'Judge not' (Matthew 7:1). He knew. He said, 'God sent not his son into the world to condemn the world' (John 3:17). He said this in times when court procedures were simple

71

and straightforward — if a man stole or killed, he was condemned. Mitigating circumstances were not taken into account. Jesus' attitude was scientific long before the conception of human behavioral science.

The whole scientific method — unbiased, exact and thorough investigation, based on facts alone, comes from Jesus. In a world of unrestrained passions, He said 'We speak that we do know, and testify that we have seen' (John 3:11), so much, nothing more, exactly like in a scientific laboratory. 'Go and show John those things which ye do hear and see' (Matthew 11:4). No fantasy, not even religious fantasy, only the observed facts, just like a scientist gathers data.

Jesus taught mankind to study what happens in nature: 'Behold the fowls of the air,' and 'Consider the lilies of the fields' (Matthew 6:26–28). From the birds men learned aviation, and from the lilies they learned botany and agronomy.

Never regard science as a danger for religion. Einstein, a scientist whose name the whole world respects, has written, 'Science without religion is lame; religion without science is blind.'

The great difference between science and religion is that the first does not establish immutable truths and eternal dogmas. It approaches truth by successive approximations without ever making the claim to complete accuracy. Religion has a definitive revelation from God — Heaven and earth will pass away, but Jesus' words will stand forever.

34: How to read the Bible

In prison we repented of many sins. We repented also of the manner in which we had read the Bible.

The Talmud fixes a rule, 'Ein dorshim maase bereshith beshanaim' — 'You do not speak about Genesis, the things of the beginning when you are in two.' God created the universe all alone. Adam was one single man. The Bible is read properly only when you transpose yourself completely into the situation and state of spirit of the author at the moment of writing.

Remember the Bible is only a summary. Adam lived 930 years, but the Bible has only one chapter and a half, 40 verses, to devote to so long a life.

Just as Cuvier reconstructed the skeleton of a prehistoric animal from a single bone, we are called upon to re-create everything from just a few words.

Remember that much of the Bible is poetry. Although Hebrew poetry does not rhyme, one of its characteristics is an alphabetical structure, e.g. Job 13:7–11, in which every line starts with an 'H.' The whole Psalm 119 is arranged alphabetically, beginning with verses which have 'a' as first letter, others which have 'b' and so on. Poetry can reveal truth, but not necessarily accuracy of detail.

The Bible is meant to be read very slowly with special pauses for respiration and meditation. In the Hebrew text there is the *athnach*, a sign which divides a verse into main clauses. Another sign for pausing is the *segholta* ∴ which subdivides the clause before *athnach*. I Kings 13:18, read according to Hebrew punctuation, would be as follows: 'And he said unto him, I am also a prophet as thou art (segoltha — a pause. Breathe and reflect) and an angel spoke unto me by the word of the Lord (the angel would not speak to you, reader, unless you pause as prescribed for meditating and evoking him),

73

saying, bring him back with thee into thine house, that he may eat bread and drink water (athnach — deep respiration, meditation). But he lied unto him. (Pause. Here there is a sign called *silluq*, which separates this verse from the following.)

Zaqeph-qaton (written:) stands for a slight pause. 'And now thus says Jehovah thy creator, O Jacob (Zaqeph-qaton, a slight pause) and thy former, O Israel (Athnach, big pause), thou shalt not fear for I have redeemed thee (slight pause), I have called by thy name, mine thou art (stop before passing to the next verse.) The Zaqeph gadol plays the role of the zaqeph-qaton where no conjunctive accent precedes.

It is good to know all this. The accents can reveal the interpretation of doubtful passages, as in Isaiah 40:3: 'The voice of one that cries (zaqeph-qaton, pause) in the wilderness (zaqeph-gadol, pause) prepare ye the way of the Lord.' Wherever two Zaqephs occur in the same clause, that which comes first is stronger. We must therefore read, 'The voice of one that cries: In the wilderness prepare ye the way of the Lord' and not, as it is usually punctuated, 'The voice of one that cries in the wilderness: prepare ye the way of he Lord.'

Learn to read the Bible slowly, breathing rhythmically, with pauses to put in the correct accents. In this way you can immerse yourself in the Spirit in which the Bible was written, and thus be able to participate in the Oneness which is its essence.

35: Open Space

Some people complain about sermons and devotional books that they are not dense enough, that they should contain more teaching. This is like complaining about a love letter that too much paper is wasted on empty spaces.

When a lover once complained about this, the black letters grew and grew to satisfy him until the sheet of paper was totally black.

Woe to a religious book which leaves no place for questions. If matter, the physical universe, is mysterious, the more so God. Man has to search. He cannot be given pre-masticated food.

It is good to ask questions in religion, but you must ask the right ones. Herod inquired of the wise men (Matthew 2:7) what time the star appeared which heralded the birth of Jesus. He did not ask how they knew that the star had anything to do with the appearance of the Messiah.

After the Lord told the parable of the sower (Matthew 13:3–8), the disciples asked, 'Why speakest thou unto them in parables?' rather than asking the more important question about why men's destinies differ so greatly and what can be done to change them.

Seeing the senselessness of many question, Jesus did not answer them. Jesus revealed what people needed to know, not what they asked for.

For many years I thought that I believed the whole Bible to be the Word of God. When I was in prison, I discovered that my belief was incomplete. The Bible consists of white sheets of paper inscribed with black letters. I had believed only the black letters to be the word of God. But there is meaning in the blank spaces, too.

The blank space can be used for decoding the ciphered parts.

In Jeremiah 25:26 we read about Sheshach, but no adversary of Israel is known by this name. The Hebrews used a simple cipher called *Athbash* in which the first letter of the alphabet, 'a,' can be exchanged with the last letter of the Hebrew alphabet 't'; the second letter, 'b,' with the second last, 'sh,' and so on. By applying this code to the word '*Sheshach*' the result is 'Babel,' the Hebrew name for 'Babylon.' In those days Babylon was a super-power. It would have been too dangerous to denounce it openly, so a nickname was used.

Many things in the Bible are coded. There are stories of sins and salvation of persons thousands of years and thousands of miles apart. Decode! You might find that you yourself are meant and are called by a code name.

There are numerous contradictions between Bible texts — Luke 9:3 forbids the apostles to carry staves, Mark 6:8 allows it; Luke 10:6 forbids sandals, Mark 6:9 allows. Many other things are sometimes allowed and sometimes forbidden. You have to find out which Bible verse applies to you at a certain moment, what things are allowed or forbidden you. There is plenty of place in the white places of the Bible for your notes and thoughts. When you have found sure guidance from God, it will be part of his eternal Word, the part for you for that given moment.

36: Oneness

For many years I was one person alone in a cell.

God is also one, and we are created in the image of God, the image of His oneness (Genesis 1:26). It is written, 'Hear, O Israel, the Lord our God is one Lord'

(Deuteronomy 6:4). The chosen people of God are one. We read 'Who is like your people Israel, a nation that is *one* in the earth' (I Chronicles 17:21 according to original). Except for God and his people, oneness is nowhere to be found, yet without it, there is no Godhead, nor can the real church exist.

Oneness creates a special state of spirit. The Jews sing, *Huh echad veein sheni*. 'He is one and there is no second.' This applies to the oneness of the children of God, too. The believer being one, without division in knower, known and act of knowledge, becomes a deep mystery for himself. Moses and Aaron said, 'What are we?' (Exodus 16:8). They did not know. Likewise, David asks, 'Who am I and what is my life?' (I Samuel 18:18).

Live in oneness, without self-contemplation, self-admiration, self-despite or self-pity. No one exists apart from this one self, no one to admire or despise you or recognize in you that your self is being despised or praised. It is a simple, serene existence. No winds blow, no tempests arise.

Deify yourself, become godlike in oneness and you will be one in the spirit with all who do likewise. It is written, 'You shall take on the first day (of the feast of tabernacles) the boughs of goodly trees, branches of palm trees and the boughs of thick trees and willows of the brook' (Leviticus 23:40).

All of these references to boughs and branches refer to Israel. Just as the citron has both taste and fragrance, so does Israel have men who are both learned and righteous in actions. Just as the fig has a taste but no fragrance, so Israel has men who have learning, but no good deeds. As the myrtle has fragrance but no flavor, so has Israel men who do good works but are not learned. And just as the willow has neither taste nor fragrance, so Israel has men who are neither learned nor righteous. And what does the Holy One, praised be He, do with them? He said, 'Let them be interrelated, united in one group, and they will be able to atone for one another.

When Israel does so, it will be exalted' (Leviticus Rabbah 30:2).

Oneness in the Church is achieved through mutual forbearance, mutual compensation.

37: Where and what is God?

A Jewish book of mysticism, 'The Zohar' writes, 'The creatures of the earth think of Him as being on high, declaring "His glory is above the heavens" ' (Psalm 113:4) while the heavenly beings think of Him as being below, declaring 'Thy glory is above all the earth' (Psalm 57:2).

Both have limited vision. God is outside of space. The One who is all in all cannot have a certain place to dwell, to the exclusion of other places. Therefore Christ who is God says, 'The foxes have holes and the birds of the air have nests; but the Son of man has not where to lay his head' (Matthew 8:20). If He were limited to space, He would not belong to Godhead.

God occupies no place anywhere. Creator of the universe, which has space as one of its attributes, He existed before there was such a thing as place. Space is required by material objects, but not by thoughts, ideals and desires which do not rest in a point fixed by geographical coordinates. God is spirit, not a material object which must exist somewhere. When the Bible says that He is in heaven, it is to indicate his elevation. God dwells in Israel, in Zion, in his Church: such things are said for the purpose of giving honor to an institution or a people. But these assertions in the Bible are never exclusive —

they do not limit God. They do not mean that He is in Zion, but not in Britain; in church, but not in a factory.

Nor can time be applied to God. The Biblical Hebrew has no tenses to indicate time; you cannot say that things have been, are or will be. You enter the sphere of Divinity, of timelessness. The Hebrew verb has only two fundamental categories, the perfect and the imperfect. *Oseh* means 'in the process of being done.' *Asah* indicates completed action. Biblical Greek also has a verb form called *Aorist*, which literally translated means 'without horizon.' God is the Creator of the universe, which has time as one of its attributes but He and his people are timeless. He was when there was no time. He will be when 'there should be time no longer' (Revelation 10:6).

God is called Father and King because we humans associate these titles with our concept of esteem. He did not procreate us as a father did. He did not become king by inheritance or conquest as other kings do. He is above all that we can say in human words.

When Livingstone went to the cannibals, he wished to teach them 'God is love,' but they did not have the word 'love.' So he asked them what was the best thing they knew. They replied 'Unboy,' which is the smoked meat from the arm of a man. So Livingstone preached, 'God is the best unboy.' He was criticized for this, but wrongly. God is not unboy, it is true, but neither is He love. Love is a sentiment shared by humans and superior animals. But is God merely a human sentiment? Because love was the highest thing the Greeks knew, John said, 'God is love,' just as Livingstone said, 'God is unboy' for those who knew no better.

There are no human words and categories to indicate how and where God is. Whenever attributes are applied to God, they are what is called 'anthropomorphisms,' likenesses from human life which are used to tell something about him. We are limited in our thoughts and words about God, but let us know that, beyond all our limitations, He is.

38: Why did Jesus change water into wine?

I spent many years among criminals, hearing from them of all the debacles that alcoholism produces. I, had I such power, would change all the alcoholic beverages into water. Why did Jesus do the opposite and change water into wine at the marriage feast in Cana? (John 2:7–11).

The word 'wine' in Biblical times did not mean what it means today. Natural fermentation produces a maximum of only 14% alcohol. Higher alcoholic content kills the yeast cell which produces it. Modern alcoholic beverages which are 50% or more alcohol are a result of freezing and distillation processes unknown in antiquity. In ancient Palestine, wine contained no more than 8% alcohol because of the limited amount of natural sugar in grape juice. The Jews had no sugar cane and so could not add sugar.

A second consideration is that both the English Bible and the Greek New Testament translate two different Hebrew words as 'wine' or, in Greek, 'oinos.'

(1) *Tirosh* occurs 38 times and has correctly been translated into Latin as 'must' or 'fresh wine.' This word probably does not refer to a fermented drink, but indicates rather a fresh fruit of the harvest as in the expression 'corn, wine and oil.' In Joel 2:24, Hosea 9:2 and Proverbs 3:10, *tirosh* is said to be filling the presses, so it could not be anything other than grape juice freshly squeezed. Isaiah speaks about 'tirosh' as 'found in the cluster.' I cannot understand how translators could use the 'wine' for a juice still in the cluster. Micah said, 'Thou shalt tread . . . *tirosh*' (6:15), which cannot possibly be considered as wine.

(2) *Yayin* occurs 153 times and means fermented

wine, but with a limited percentage of alcohol as explained above.

If the story of the events in Cana is translated so that Jesus changed water into *must*, it would be more consistent with the condemnation of drunkenness and the commandment of sobriety so often repeated in the Bible.

39: Daring arguments with God

Saints have sometimes dared to argue with God. And sometimes they have won. When God decided to destroy the Jewish people because they were worshipping the golden calf, Moses said to Him, 'Turn from thy fierce wrath and repent of this evil against thy people. . . . And the Lord repented of the evil which he thought to do unto his people' (Exodus 32:14).

Job accused God of laughing at the trial of the innocent and giving the earth into the hand of the wicked (9:23–24). David prayed in despair, 'How long wilt thou forget me, O Lord?' (Psalm 8:13).

The Lord said to Cain (after the latter killed Abel) 'Where is Abel, your brother?' He answered, 'I do not know. Am I my brother's keeper?' (Genesis 4:9). Cain was, in effect, saying 'You, O Lord, are the Keeper, the one who should watch over all creatures, and yet You ask me concerning Abel.' This situation may be compared to that of a thief whose burglary escaped noticed until morning. When the watchman caught him, he asked, 'Why did you steal?' The thief answered, 'I am a thief by profession, and I do my work regularly. Your profession is to stand watch at the gate. Why did you abandon your profession? And now you ask me why I stole!' Thus, too, did Cain speak to God: 'I killed Abel; but You created in me the impulse to evil. You are the Keeper of all and yet You permitted me to kill him. *You* have killed him! If you had accepted my offering as You accepted his, I would not have been jealous of him' (From the Midrash).

A man once came to a pastor for advice. 'What should I do about blasphemous thoughts which pass through my mind?' he said. 'I am assailed by the idea that there is no God and that if he does exist, he is not good. This drives me to madness because if this were the case, the world and life would be entirely senseless. How could we continue to be in a world without a good God?' The pastor answered 'Do not fear. Just go on with your "blasphemous" thoughts.'

Rabbi Elimelekh of Lizhensk once sent his disciples on the eve of the Day of Atonement to observe the actions of a tailor. 'From him,' he said, 'you will learn what a man should do on this holy day.' From a window they saw the tailor take a book from his shelf in which was written all the sins that he had committed throughout the year. Book in hand, the tailor addressed God: 'Today, the day of forgiveness for all Israel, the moment has come for us — You, God, and myself — to settle our account. Here is the list of all my sins, but here also is another volume in which I have written down all the sins that You have committed, the pain, the woe and the heartache that You have sent me and my family. Lord of the universe, if we were to total the accounts exactly, You would owe me much more than I would owe You! But it is the eve of the Day of Atonement, when everyone is commanded to make peace with his fellow. Hence, I forgive You for your sins if You will forgive me for mine.' the tailor then poured himself a cup of wine, pronounced the blessing over it, and then exclaimed: 'L'hayyim! (To life!), Master of the world. Let there now be peace and joy between us, for we have forgiven each other, and our sins are now as if they never were.'

82

The disciples returned to Rabbi Elimelekh, recounted what they had seen and heard and complained that the tailor's words were overly impudent before Heaven. Their master answered that God Himself and His heavenly court had come to listen to what the tailor had said in great simplicity, and the tailor's words had caused great joy in all the spheres.

Speak with God as with a friend. You can prevail over him. If you consider something he does unjust, say so. Do not cover your inner complaints with flatteries which are not sincere.

God had decided that only males would inherit in Israel. The daughters of Telephehad pleaded with Moses to return to God and to tell him that since their father had no sons, the law should not apply to them. They should inherit, even though they were females. Moses returned with God's answer, 'The daughters of Telephehad speak right' (Numbers 27:7).

Be daring with God. Not all his decrees are definitive. Through clearly expressing your dissatisfactions and doubts, you may receive understanding.

40: El — a name of God

Hebrew is a unique tongue — spare, lean, sinewy, yet rich, even poetic. Built around a skeleton of a mere four hundred roots, it impresses when flashed out. Able to bear heavy burdens of thought, it flexes its musculature with great subtlety and hides the secrets of its skill from all but the learned or enlightened.

Many languages contain homonyms, but none so many as the Semitic tongues. Yet the different meanings of a word must have a connection between them in the deeper layers of our psyche, or men would not have chosen to use the same vehicle for different notions.

Therefore, by translating a given Hebrew word into its English equivalent, one does not carry across the whole truth, since in Hebrew, as in several other Semitic idioms, a word has not one but a cluster of meanings. In the Chicago Assyrian dictionary, for instance, eight pages were needed to relate all the possible interpretations of the Semitic word *abu*.

A modern illustration of this clustering of meanings (in this case, among homonyms) comes to mind. Sigmund Freud once wrote of a German psychotic who was obsessed with the idea that rats (*Ratten* in German) were attacking him. Under psychoanalysis it was established that he was worried about two things: he could not pay the installments (in German, *Raten*) on his house, and because of this he was not able to marry (in German, *hei-raten*). These concerns, exhibiting themselves in similar words, were behind his obsession with rats.

Likewise, with Semitic languages words with the same or similar sounds are related to each, though more deeply, strongly, or expressively than is the case with our modern European languages.

We must keep these subsurface relationships in mind in order to understand *El*, a name frequently used for 'God' in the Hebrew Bible. (The corresponding Sumerian and Ugaritic name for God is *Il*.) In the original Hebrew text of the Old Testament there were no vowels. The name *El* was written with the letters *Alef*, a mute sound, and *L*. Therefore, 'El' is not the only possible pronunciation of these two letters: they are sometimes pronounced 'Al.'

As 'El' they meant 'God,' 'toward,' or 'against'; as 'Al' they meant a mild prohibition, a negative wish, like the Greek *me*. We find this 'Al' in I Samuel 22:15: 'Let not the king impute anything . . .' It is obvious that nobody could give the king an order, so the word 'Al' is substituted for an absolute command. It is used only with the so-called jussive form of the verb, which is a semi-command.

When a Hebrew pronounced or read a word, all its possible connotations collaborated in producing an impression upon him, just as a chord struck on a piano, sets up sympathetic vibrations in every other stringed instrument within range. Likewise, when he approached God *El*, he knew he was approaching a mysterious being Who cannot be reached in this life but Who always remains a direction 'toward' — *El* — which one moves.

In addition, the one who worships Him automatically becomes a man who is 'against' — the same word *El*. Henceforth he must swim against the stream. Christians, wrote Paul, are not conformed to this world (Rom. 12:2). They know which way the wind blows, but they follow their own course.

The moment one calls upon God *El*, another string vibrates: 'Al' — the discreet advice, 'Please don't!' A relationship with God includes, then, acceptance of the 'Al,' of His plea, 'Don't rush to do this thing you have in mind.' It also invites recognition of the fact that He never spoke against an action unless it was harmful to the individual or to society.

Rabbi Pinhas of Korez once spoke these mysterious words: 'People think they pray to God, but it is not so. For the prayer itself is the essence of Godhead.' The meaning is clear when one understands that in Hebrew *El* signifies the aim, God, as well as the directing of the heart to Him. Prayer is *El* just as the Person to Whom one prays is *El*. Thus, 'Toward' and 'God' are the same word in divine revelation.

It behooves us, then, to pronounce *El*, the name of God, bearing all this in mind. Let us repeat it with love . . . *El*. Just as the name of an earthly beloved — of a bride, of a child, of a sweetheart — brings honey to the mouth, so the names of the Lord, infused with His glory, are sweet.

The Lord taught His disciples to pray, 'Hallowed be Thy name' (Matt. 5:9). Summarizing His work on earth that last evening before Gethsemane and Golgotha, He said to His Father, 'I have manifested Thy name' (John 17:6). If we pronounce His name with piety and devotion, our eyes will behold His attributes and His wonderful works.

Often we use the word 'God' casually, without reverence. Not so the Jews who, when they write the scroll of the Law for the synagogue, immerse in water for purification as often as they come to one of His names. If they write it fifty times a day, they immerse fifty times — sometimes, in winter, in icy water.

In an acorn resides the oak. In the short name *El*, Godhead itself lives. Pronouncing His name with devotion helps to unite our mind with His and enlarge our understanding.

Between us and our names there is often a difference. A human being can have the name of Mary without being pure; the name of Magdalene without watching faithfully at the foot of His cross; the name of Paul without being an apostle; the name of Richard without having a lion-heart. With God the difference between Himself and His name does not exist. We magnify Him when we magnify His name. He speaks through us when we have His name reverently on our lips.

If the names of God are a flight of steps leading to God Himself, *El* is the first step. Flies buzz indiscriminately from blossoms to dunghills, bees only from flower to flower. So we should move from one name of God to another, settling from time to time also on His commandments, precepts, miracles, and on His life as reflected in His saints.

The Moslem 'Allah' is not the same as *El*. Allah refers only to the Creator and no one else. The Hebrew 'El,' as well as 'Elohim,' another name, like the word 'god' in English, was used also for men. God said to Moses, 'Thou shalt be to Pharaoh instead of God' (Exodus 4:16). Jesus said to His Jewish audience, quoting the Psalmist, 'Is it not written in your law, I said, Ye are gods? (John

10:34). He called them gods 'unto whom the word of God came.'

If we seek earnestly to know God-*El* and speak His holy name with reverence, we too may find ourselves, in time, individuals toward whom the desires of many turn. Our loving words and our meek 'don'ts' will have value. We may even become symbols to those who are against unrighteousness. Such are the gracious significations included in the seminal holy syllable

El.

41: Compounds names of God

'Tao [God] named is not the real Tao,' said Lao-Tse, and there is truth in this assertion.

The possibility of giving names to any thing or person, including God, is circumscribed by the limitations of language itself. First of all, a given language has a certain number of letters or characters at its disposal in the formation of words. Suppose, for instance, that God had a name requiring for its expression an English 'w,' a Spanish 'ñ' (as in *mañana*), or a German 'ö.' Such a name would not have been accessible to the Hebrews because their language contained neither these sounds nor their corresponding letters. By the same token, the Hebrew name of Jesus — *Jeshua* — cannot be written accurately in English.

Second, the potential for giving names depends on the available substantives, verbs, adjectives, and so on, of a language. The aggregate is called in Sanskrit *nāmān*, from which the Greeks derived *anoma* and the English *name*. The name of God, then, is the sum total of words in which His character can be expressed. Thus, when you pray, as Jesus enjoined in the Lord's Prayer, 'Hallowed be Thy name,' recognize its limitations. Look to the reality for which there are no names in our language, the real Person beyond any name in any tongue.

Because no name is complete or all-embracing, there are many names for God in Scripture. The Son of God could be called in Hebrew 'the lamb' or 'the lion of Judah.' But when He was introduced to the Eskimos, these names were meaningless, since they had no knowledge of such animals. Other names had to be found.

One should be wary of confounding a name with identification. God has many aliases because every name of His is only an approximation.

Even the word 'name' has a double sense in Hebrew. The corresponding word is *Shem*. Now, Shem is one of the sons of Noah and the progenitor of the Semitic race. In Scripture his name stands for the Semites, just as Japheth stands for the Indo-German race descended from him (Genesis 9:27). When Jesus taught His Jewish disciples the 'Our Father' and said '*Jitgadal shimcha*,' We have here a typical example of how ideas reduced to words can be exposed to different interpretations. The words can be correctly translated 'Hallowed be thy name' and 'Hallowed be thy semitic race'. He who wishes to hallow God must of necessity approach Him as He is, beyond words.

To overcome this difficulty, the Bible provides not only simple names of God such as El, Elohim, JHWH (Jahweh, or Jehovah), but also compound names, just as in mathematics one uses not only whole numbers but also decimals to arrive closer to reality.

For instance, the Lord appeared to Abraham as *El-Shaddai* (Genesis 17:1), which means 'a sufficient God,' 'a nurturing God,' or more literally 'God — a female breast,' that is, a God who feeds one at His breast.

The English Authorized Version says, 'I am the Lord that heals thee' (Exodus 15:26). But the Hebrew uses only two words, a compound name of God, '*Jehovah-Rophe*,' the healing Jehovah. Furthermore, the Hebrew does not contain the idea that he heals '*thee*.' God does not revolve around your person. He simply heals.

'*Jehovah-Jireh*' (Genesis 22:14) means literally 'God who sees to it or who provides.' '*Jehovah-Megaddesh*' (Leviticus 20:8) is God who renews or sanctifies. '*Jehovah-Shalom*' (Judges 6:24) is God-peace.

'*Jehovah-nissi*' (Exodus 17:15) means 'God — my wonder' or 'God — my sign.' This compound name is also the name of an altar built to God, to indicate that approaching the altar can signify approaching God Himself.

The name '*Jehovah-Tsidkenu*' (Jeremiah 23:6), meaning 'God — our righteousness,' belongs not only to Godhead, but also to His people, since the Jewish nation is called by this name. Thus, to join His flock is like joining God.

One interesting compound name is '*Jehovah-shammah*' (Ezekiel 48:35), meaning 'God is there.' In Hebrew, 'there' when applied to a male subject is *sham*, when applied to a female is *shammah*. Here is a case in which the name of Jehovah is linked to a female substantive, indicating the all-encompassing nature of His love and concern for His creatures.

The names by which a sovereign God deigns to be called in Scripture to reveal His character to humanity are many and varied and could inspire volumes. Their very multiplicity underscores the difficulty of reducing Godhead to the limitations of human language. But they are intended to reveal to sinful man the many facets of a loving God.

How sad it would be for a lover to know only the name of his beloved, when he desires the beloved herself. To sanctify the name of God — to pray 'Hallowed be Thy name' — means to advance from knowledge *about* God to the blessed reality of His presence.

42: Anohi and Ani

There is often little resemblance between the peoples and the languages they speak. Missionaries who have lived among primitive tribes sometimes found, to their surprise, that the native languages were far ahead of the natives. The language bore the stamp of thought and development.

The grammar of the Ambrim tribe in the New Hebrides is more precise than that of English. *Ire* is an 'inclusive we,' comprising both speaker and the person spoken to. *Komai* is an 'exclusive we,' in which the person spoken to is not included. In a sermon, 'Our Father' would be used with the inclusive pronoun, to include the congregation; but when the preacher prays, 'Our Father,' he would use the exclusive pronoun so as to exclude God, the person addressed.

The uncultured, degraded Jews, who had emerged from 400 years of slavery, had a highly developed language, such as you would not have expected in a nation at that level.

There are two Hebrew expressions for 'I': *Ani* and *Anohi*. *Ani* emphasizes the pronoun. It is used when one boasts '*I* did it.' When attention is focused upon the action rather than on the person who performed it, the expression *Anohi*, in the sense 'I *did* it!', is used.

The Ten Commandments begin with the words *Anohi Adonai Eloheiha* (Exodus 20:2), which shows that the sentence is to be read 'I *am* the Lord thy God.' The emphasis is not 'I' but that the Lord *is* our God, a God who has freed people from slavery and wishes to free us, too; a Lord on whom we can rely.

The words of Cecil Rhodes, the founder of the British Empire in Southern Africa, were, 'So much to do; so little done.' He had been a man for whom it was important that great achievements of the English should be

accomplished through *him*. Although he had had fore-
runners, and others would continue his work, this could
not satisfy him. He passed away feeling that *he* had done
little. Rhodes would have used *Ani* to refer to himself.

The Christian or divine manner of thinking is just the
contrary. The *Ani* disappears in *Anohi*. The self is denied
(Luke 9:23). The work to which we are called is what
is important. We do our little part. We are happy if
others do even more and better than we.

The whole structure of the Hebrew language de-em-
phasizes the role of the individual, putting the accent on
the deed performed. The English sentence 'Moses
guarded a horse,' which tells us what Moses did, can be
translated in Hebrew only as *Shamar Mosheh sus* —
'Guarded Moses a horse.' The important thing is the
guarding of the horse. That this was done by Moses was
of secondary importance.

Even the first verse of the Bible sounds different in
Hebrew than in English. In English the emphasis is on
God. 'In the beginning *God* created.' We are meant to
know that the universe is His doing and we should adore
Him. In the Hebrew the emphasis is that in the beginning God *created* the heavens and the earth. The order
of the words in the original Genesis 1:1 is 'In the beginning created God.' Rejoice in the beauty of creation —
this is the primary meaning. The Hebrew text satisfies
also one's curiosity about who is behind it. It was created
by a God who keeps himself in humility.

Such nuances as *Ani* and *Anohi* or putting the verb
before the subject show how important the manner of
reading the Bible is. The Master asks a lawyer, 'How do
you read?' It is obviously not the same thing to read '*I*
and the Father are one,' 'I *and* the Father are one,' 'I
and the *Father* are one,' 'I and the Father *are* one,' or
'I and the Father are *one*.'

In reading the Bible, much depends upon the voice
and intonation. I have met only once in my life (in
Finland) a pastor who recited from memory the Bible
text for the sermon so convincingly that the sermon

91

which followed was superfluous. The Bible reading had already brought souls to conversion and illumination.

Let us learn to think in the Hebrew manner even though speaking another language. De-emphasise the self; focus on the action performed.

43: The Keri and the Ketib

In the 10th century A.D., the Masoretes, a number of authoritative rabbis, established ancient rules in writing for the proper transcription and reading of the Old Testament. Besides certain alterations in spelling and wording due to the addition of vowels which did not originally exist, the present text also contains the musical notations for chanting the Scriptures, along with some strange annotations called *Keri* or 'the reading' as distinguished from *Ketib*, 'the writing.'

The Masoretes established that certain words were to be written one way, but read another. The simple written text veiled certain mysteries of the Bible. Often a simple story contains details which seem irrelevant, but are actually secret meanings which lie beneath the surface in coded language. The *Keri* is the key for unlocking the code and revealing the deeper meaning of the story.

A case of Keri versus Ketib is found in II Kings 5:12 in which Naaman the leper asks, 'Are not *Abana* and *Pharpar*, rivers of Damascus, better than all the waters of Israel?' It would be difficult to prove any sort of qualitative difference between the rivers of Palestine and Syria, nor can we definitely identify any Syrian rivers by these names. But the Keri of the Masoretic text soon reveals the hidden meaning by changing the spelling of

the 'rivers' to read: 'Are not *Amanah* and *Parpar* better?'
Soon the hidden meaning becomes clear.

Hebrew words often have male and female forms, like
the male and female substantives in German and Latin.
Amanah is the female form of *Amen*. It connotes complete female submission, saying 'Amen' to all the Divine
spouse has decided. *Par* is an animal brought as sacrifice
and *parpar* is thus superlative sacrifice. Naaman's question may now be understood in its deeper sense: 'Is not
saying a superlative "Amen" (complete submission to
God's will, as exemplified by virgin Mary's acceptance
of the angel's decree that she become the mother of the
Lord), and offering valuable sacrifices — are these not
more worthy than washing in the River Jordan?'

The most obvious answer is 'yes.' But when God commands something ordinary or common, simple obedience
assumes a higher aspect, and may become worthier in
God's eyes than an action that may seem more valuable.
Many would be ready to do great works for the Lord,
but would not be willing to humbly scrub the floor of an
orphanage or mission-office. Naaman was not required
to seek a high spiritual action, such as the saying of
Amanah or bringing of *Parpar*. The leper had to do
something common: to wash himself in the Jordan, because that was God's will for him. May we learn from
the revealed meaning of this story!

44: How to speak

I regretted in jail the manner in which I had previously preached. The Hebrew word for 'to speak,' 'leomer,' implies the notion 'to speak excellently.' The speech of a child of God cannot be other than excellent. Hence, the expression 'to speak excellently' would be a tautology in Biblical Hebrew. 'Leomer' is also used in Biblical Hebrew for 'to command.'

When Jesus spoke he spoke excellently, commandingly, whereas most men only chatter. He spoke in beautiful parables, in a noble manner, and his followers spoke nobly also. The following parable illustrates how believers learned the secret of 'leomer' from Christ.

A wise king asked a renowned painter whether he could paint a dragon for him. Happy to serve the king, the painter replied, 'Certainly.' The king then asked him, 'But have you ever seen a dragon?' As the painter had not, the king advised him, 'Seek first to see a dragon and paint it afterward.' The painter knew that dragons were mythical figures, and reflected about the meaning of the king's order. He thought, 'The king must have meant I should first look for a man as evil as a dragon.' So he went from jail to jail until he found a fierce criminal, whose very appearance breathed murder. He returned to the king and told him, 'I am ready to paint. I have seen a dragon.' The king inquired, 'Does this dragon appeal to you?' 'No,' replied the painter. 'Go again,' said the king, 'and find a dragon which attracts rather than frightens you.' After years passed in meditation, the painter returned to the king and said, 'I found the dragon you mentioned in my own bosom. It is my own wicked heart. I will paint it.' And he painted his self portrait.

The beauty of this parable shows that those who

understood it had learned from Jesus to comprehend the Hebrew manner of speaking exquisitely.

Jesus *says*, (meaning that He spoke the following words in the most beautiful and compelling way), 'From within, out of the heart of men, proceed evil thoughts, adulteries, fornications, murders, thefts, covetousness, wickedness, deceit, lasciviousness, the evil eye, blasphemy, pride, foolishness' (Mark 7:21–22). Christ said this long before the psychoanalysts and more beautifully and powerfully than they. And in the same sublime manner, He said that the remedy for the evils within the human heart is 'the blood of the New Testament, which is shed for many of the remission of sins' (Matthew 26:28).

It was said about Jesus, 'Never man spoke like this man' (John 7:46). He spoke excellently, in accord with the genius of his language. Let us also learn to speak exquisitely and in a manner which gives pleasure.

45: Jesus' multiple crucifixions

Several places in Jerusalem are shown as having been the site of Golgatha. This is as it should be, for there have been a multitude of Golgathas. Jesus was not crucified only once.

Sculptors and painters have tried to help us encounter the crucifixion that occurred 2,000 years ago. But Jesus suffers even more cruelly today when those who were once enlightened fall away and 'crucify to themselves the Son of God afresh' (Hebrews 6:4–6).

A mass falling-away, the great apostasy, is taking place

today, just as was prophesied for the days before Christ's coming again. Today's crucifixions occur as a mass phenomenon. It is not just a few hundred people shouting, 'Crucify Him'; not just a small band of soldiers flogging Him and hammering nails into His flesh. Now millions participate. And they are crucifying a glorified Lord, one who is in heaven where the anguish of heart for the eternal fate of mankind is much more intense than on earth.

Charles Gardiner, famous mining engineer in South Africa once refused to dismount from his horse to examine some gold which was being shown to him. He said, 'Earth of this chemical composition cannot contain gold.' Walker, a carpenter who discovered a reef whose contents in gold and diamonds was assessed at 3 billion dollars, died in poverty because he thought the diamonds were merely shining toys for children. Unenlightened men often pass by things of high value without giving them due importance. This is forgiven without much ado.

But once you have been enlightened, be careful; tremble once you have tasted the heavenly gift, fear once you are a partaker of the Holy Ghost. To taste the Word of God and the powers of the world to come is a great responsibility. Henceforth, by abandoning your faith, you become one of the henchmen who crucify the Son of God afresh, this time a glorified Son of God (Hebrews 6.6).

The first crucifixion, though a horrible crime, brought salvation to mankind. Your fresh crucifixion of the Lord may also prove beneficent in some way — everything concurs to the good in the wise plan of God — but the Church will no longer be able to renew *you* to repentance. Beware!

While others crucify Him afresh, my aim in life is to de-crucify Him. Will you join me in this?

In order to de-crucify Him you must forget about yourself.

Once there was a saintly monk who prayed a great deal but also spent much time caring for the beard of

96

which he was quite proud. An angel appeared with the message that this was displeasing to God, and that the beard should be sacrified. The monk was humbled and immediately accepted the reproach. Carefully he plucked out his beard, hair by hair. Now, every time he prayed, he thought with satisfaction about the fact that he had given up his beard. The angel appeared again and told him sadly, 'Nothing has changed. Your mind still dwells upon your beard.'

Abandon what is good within you as utterly as you forsake the evil within you. May He, and only He, live in you. By so doing you de-crucify Jesus.

46: The Jesus

One of the strange things in the Gospel is that sometimes the definite article is placed before the names of Jesus, Peter, and other personalities, as if these were not proper names.

It is most irregular to place the definite article before a proper name. I would not refer to my wife as 'the Sabine' or to my son as 'the Michael.' Usually an article is placed only before a generic name, e.g., 'the Christian,' or 'the believer.' It is as if the Evangelists intended to portray certain types rather than real persons.

'The Jesus' (*ho Iisus* in Greek), is the prototype of 'the Jesus-type man,' who responds to certain circumstances in a certain manner according to a spiritual law. Similarly there is 'the Peter-type man,' and the 'Pilate-type.'

In Hebrew, even the spelling of the name changes when the definite article is placed before it. 'The' in Hebrew is *ha*. After this prefix the first letter of a name or noun is doubled. Jesus in Hebrew is *Yeshuah*; *'The Jesus'* would be *Ha-Yyeshuah*. 'The Peter' would be 'Happetrus.'

The Greek article or this little prefix *ha* in Hebrew have great depth and can be a matter for much fruitful mediation.

In his splendid collections of sufite stories, Indries Shah tells of a Moslem monk who attended religious discussions, listening attentively to all that was said, but always remaining silent. People wondered why he came and considered him too stupid to understand their debates. One day the monk invited the others to visit his monastery. They were brought to a grand marble building, splendidly carpeted, with dervishes everywhere in meditation. These rose and bowed respectfully when the monk appeared. The guests realized how they had erred in thinking disdainfully about their host. After a good meal, the guests were given pleasant rooms for sleep. When they awoke, the monastery was gone. They had been sleeping on a mountain top, on stones, and were half frozen. They cursed the monk who, through some magic, had made them believe in the existence of the luxurious temple, and they worried about how to get down from the mountain. But all at once they found themselves at their usual gathering in one of their homes, where religious matters were heatedly being debated. The monk sat in the corner as usual, without saying a word.

The people fell upon him, demanding an explanation. He said, 'You are caught in deceit. You are not able to distinguish truth from falsehood. Otherwise you would be quiet and sure, knowing the truth only for living, and not as subject for debate. Would you debate $2 \times 2 = 4$? You have accepted on illusion after another; a monastery all of marble, then a hostile mountaintop. Perhaps even this room and your religious discussions are simple illusions like the others.' Having spoken these words, he disappeared.

Those who belong to 'the Jesus,' to 'the Jesus-type,'

to what the Bible calls the body of Jesus, belong to it now as much as did Jesus of Nazareth 2,000 years ago. A foot is as much a part of a body as a head, requiring no discussion or debate to bring them together. 'The tribes of Israel said to David, Behold we are your bone and your flesh' (II Samuel 5:1). Christians can say the same words to Jesus Christ. When they suffer, Jesus suffers. When they are received and helped, Jesus is helped. They belong to the '*ho Iisus.*' They are no longer spectators of the life of Jesus, another person than themselves, but actors in the drama '*ho Iisus.*'

47: Kala

The Gospels have retained some of the words which our Lord spoke on the cross in the Aramaean language, e.g. '*Eloi, Eloi, lama sabahtani?*' Others are known only in the Greek translation.

One of Jesus' utterances as he died can have different meanings. This is the word, 'It is finished' (John 19:30), in the sense that the work of redemption of our sins through His shedding of blood has now been accomplished. The corresponding Hebrew word, which Jesus will have pronounced is 'Kalah' which means also 'Bride.' Could this not have been a last thought of love for Jesus' bride, the Church? Does it not perhaps show that she and her purity until His return were His last desire?

If a cry after His bride was one of our Lord's last words, we can be at peace. He will help us to overcome all our handicaps.

Isidore of Seville ran away from school, finding scholarship too difficult. Sitting down beside a spring that trickled over a rock, he watched the water as it fell in drops, one at a time. The drops had worn away a large stone. This sight inspired him with hope that his dullness could be conquered. Later he became one of the greatest scholars of his time. These drops of water gave Britain a brilliant historian, and the Church a famous teacher.

Everyone belonging to te Church, the bride of Christ, can be confident, however humble and backward he might be. For over three years Jesus was aware of the sins, doubts and misunderstandings of his apostles. Once he had to call Peter 'Satan' to bring him to his senses (Matthew 16:23). He said to them all, 'How long shall I suffer you?' (Matthew 17:17) but he loved them passionately, and, when nailed to the cross, He sighed, 'O, bride.'

The sins of believers are only temporary. 'When He shall appear, we shall be like Him' (I John 3:2). Each of us will be another aspect of Jesus, as beautiful and pure as He is.

We were His last thought. May He have pre-eminence in our lives today, and be our last thought too. May our parting word be 'Bridegroom,' as His perhaps was 'Bride.'

48: Identification with Christ

David sang, 'Thou wilt not leave my soul in hell, neither wilt Thou suffer thine Holy One to see corruption. Thou wilt show me the path of life' (Psalm 16:10–11). Peter explains in Acts 2:27–31 that the prophet was speaking these words about Christ, that is, about someone other than himself, someone who would appear on earth many centuries in the future. Why then did David use the first person, not the third, speaking about the Messiah as if He were David himself?

This is because believers and the Messiah are not two persons, but one. We are His body, 'We are of His flesh and of His bones' (Ephesians 5:30). The unity between ourselves and Christ could not have been expressed more realistically.

It can be understood figuratively that we are His flesh, but how can one explain symbolically that we are also 'His bones?' It is a common expression that the Church is the mystical body of Christ, but it is not biblical. The words 'symbolic' and 'mystic' never occur in Scriptures.

We are called *His body*, period. My body is myself. My legs do not walk: *I* walk. My lungs do not breathe: *I* breathe. It is not Christ's members who suffer or rejoice: it is always Christ Himself. The identification is complete.

David speaks about the Saviour using the first person, exactly as the Saviour uses the first person when He speaks about me, the sinner for whom He dies. Psalm 69 is also messianic. It is Christ Himself who speaks through the pen of David: 'In my thirst they gave me vinegar to drink' (v. 21), and 'the zeal of thine house has eaten me up' (v. 9).

In the same psalm, we also read the words, 'O God, thou knowest my foolishness and my sins are not hid from thee' (v. 5). Christ does not say that he will suffer ignominy for someone else's foolishness and wrongs, but for His own. He has identified with the sinner. Luther writes in his commentary to Galatians, 'the Christian is Christ.' By the same token, we could say, 'Christ is the Christian.'

Identified with Him, we must share His fate. 'In the day of trouble he shall hide me in his tent' (Psalm 27:5 according to the Hebrew). The rule established by the Jewish teachers called Masaretes for writing the 's' in the Hebrew word *sukkah*, 'tent,' is that it be exceptionally small, half the size of the other letters, to show that one who wishes to be protected by Him must accept confinement and constraint in a small place just as He himself found solace with only a little flock. (I was in a small cell with peace only for two steps to and fro.)

But the letter 'm' in *iom*, 'day,' in 'day of trouble,' is also written unusually small. For believers, days of trouble are small in comparison with the eternity of glory. We are identified with Him on His cross, but also in His victory.

49: The undivided Bible

The original manuscripts of the Old and New Testaments are not divided into chapters and verses. The first division into chapters was made by Cardinal Hugo of Santa Clara in 1250, the first division into verses, by the Parisian printer Robert Stephanus centuries later.

In its original version, the Bible is not even divided into words: a whole book of the Bible, sometimes several together constitute a single word. When Scripture is read in this manner, it makes an extraordinary impression.

In English, 'Male and female' in Genesis 1:27 evokes the picture of two separate beings who are united and can therefore also be disunited. Whatever is compounded can disintegrate. The original version reads, 'maleandfemalecreatedhethem.' 'Maleandfemale' is something so essentially united that the idea of separation is impossible to consider.

In our Bibles, we read, 'Peter and Andrew, Philip and Bartholomew, Thomas and Matthew, etc' (Matthew 10:103). The original has 'Peterandandrewphilipandbartholomewthomasandmatthew.' It is one indivisible word. There is one God who has revealed not tens of thousands of words, but only one. Not a single part can be omitted without deforming the whole and making it crumble.

The Lord's prayer, in the original, does not begin with 'Our Father,' which suggests that He might be a Father without being ours, or that He might be ours without having a fatherly relationship with us. The original reads, 'Ourfather.' We Christians, cannot conceive a god which should not be ours. He is a father toward us or He ceases to be our god. The Hebrew as used by Christ for 'our Father' was a single word, *Avinu*, the possessive pronoun being part of the whole.

A Jew came to a rabbi and asked him to pray that he might earn a decent living. 'Unite with God and you will get a livelihood,' the rabbi advised. The Jew said, 'But I do not know how to unite with God.'

The rabbi was amazed. 'You do not know how to unite with the Godhead and yet you complain about having no livelihood? You want a minor wish granted and are not worried about the major problem?'

The main thing is to realize the unity of the Godhead, 'thefatherthesonandtheholyghost,' one God expressed in one word, the unity of His revelation, the unity of reality, our unity with the whole of it and with God. Einstein's concept, 'The whole reality is one electromagnetic field,' is expressed by the manner in which the Bible is written it its early manuscripts.

50: Why such a strange book?

It is strange that for the purpose of our salvation we were given a book which is so difficult to understand, with whole chapters of boring and seemingly useless genealogies or enumerations of persons without importance. Ezra 10, for example, contains a long list of priests conspicuous only for the fact that they had taken foreign wives. The book is also repetitive with some episodes recounted three or four times. Religious writers with the inspiration and clarity of John Chrysostom of Spurgean could surely have written better literature than the Biblical authors.

The Bible is written so as not to be understood at first glance. In Acts 22:11 Paul writes about being unable to see because of the glory of the heavenly light. I have lived in dark prison cells. When I saw the light again it blinded me, and I had to readjust myself slowly. Only those who grow accustomed to dwelling in glory can understand the secrets of the Bible.

The carnal mind longs after limitation, accuracy, precise definitions and well-established borders. It shuns eternity where these things disappear. God prefers to commune with us in silence. The 30 years which Jesus spent in silence reveal more about God than what He spoke in three years.

Words express only part of reality: the best part of wisdom is that which words cannot contain. The moment a soul speaks, its inner nature is sullied by its transitory passions, interests, prejudices, surmises or theatricality. The true nature of the soul is desecrated by expression.

The Bible is not a great work of art. Rhetoric begins when the last reality has been drowned. Eloquent style is a sign of degeneration.

The lives of many great poets were unhappy because

they spoke too much. Romeo and Juliet spent their first night together declaiming poetry to each other. Could their marriage have been a happy one?

The Bible is a strange, silent caress of the bride by the Beloved. It contains words and whole chapters whose value no one can see. But this *is* their value. If a bride is reading a passionately interesting novel, filled with exciting detail and embellished with beautiful style, the bridegroom remains uncaressed. But in the Bible there are whole chapters of endless geneologies and lists of names. One grows bored and puts the book aside. This was the purpose: to put the book down sometimes and entrust yourself to the inebriating silent embrace where the problems of the text cease to exist. You have His Kiss. To prepare you to receive it is the purpose of the Holy book.

51: Bible monologues

Being in a lonely cell, for many years the only talks I knew were monologues. The Bible contains several monologues of God, for example, 'Let us make man in our image' (Genesis 1:26), or 'They will reverance my Son' (Matthew 21:37).

Let us learn from God! Speaking with oneself has a healing value. God put some of his revelations to us in the form of monologue, not because of His need for healing, but in order to teach us how to find it.

None of us is a unitary being. We are all to some degree split between conflicting tendencies in our personalities. Everyone has his ideal self or 'I,' what the psychologist Jung calls 'the animus,' and everyone has an evil urge which attracts him as well. 'The pastor Hermas,' one of the oldest Christian writings, asserts that every man has a personal devil just as he has a guardian angel. We are torn by many influences coming from opposing directions.

As often as we say a 'yes,' there is also something in us saying, 'No.' This is our inner counterpart with whom it is very important to clarify matters.

I have known men with powerful criminal instincts who overcame them by using the method of the monologue. First they proclaimed aloud to themselves their desire to commit the wrong action; then they pleaded the victim's defense, loudly crying his cry when attacked; they spoke out the reproaches of their wives and children for what they had done, the prosecutor's condemnation, and their own possible defense. At last they're determined not to do the deed.

A man was greatly troubled because he had killed an enemy in a bayonet fight during World War I. He discussed the matter with the victim within himself. He convinced his counterpart that it had been a fair fight in which both had obeyed orders and had been dedicated to the good of their respective fatherlands. He expressed his regret and promised to make restitution by adopting a child from the former enemy nation.

Whenever conscience nags or doubts haunt, it is best not to repress these voices, but to weigh the pros and cons aloud to oneself. The blood of Christ will always be sufficient for past sins. The light of the Holy Spirit will be enough to dissipate doubts.

The purpose of God's monologues differs from ours, but we can learn from Him of their value.

52: The value of willing rightly

'She said within herself' (Matthew 9:21). 'He spoke within himself' (Luke 7:39).

What is important is not so much what we say with our lips as what we say within ourselves. Whenever we speak to others we look to the consequences of what we say in case we should be held responsible. We might be drawn before court; we might lose our jobs; we can have all kinds of complications. For many reasons we do not outwardly express everything we inwardly feel.

God looks at the heart. He hears our inward speech, both good and bad, and it is according to this that He judges us.

Now a man's inward speech can be as diverse and incongruous as his outward speech. I speak within myself; I also inwardly judge what I say. I may criticize my inward speech or, at other times, approve it. Man is not of one piece. We are always torn between conflicting desires which are expressed by contradictory inner voices. Behind all this strife is the final reality within us which, observing this whole life in serenity, hears our inner talks, but remains silent. This is Christ within us, the one whom the Hindus call, 'The jewel in the lotus-flower.'

The battle must be won within. Outwardly your talk might be most edifying, but perhaps the Lord's words apply to you: 'Ye make clean the outside of the cup and of the platter, but within they are full of extortion and excess' (Matthew 23:25).

How can we make the inside clean? Simply by willing. The Lord once said to Mechthilde, 'When you have to receive my body and my blood, will for the glory of my name to have all the fervour and all the zeal which the most burning heart has ever had for me. Then you will be able to approach me trusting, having this preparation, because I will look to the fervour which you wish to have and I will take account of it as if you would really have it.'

Something similar is told of St Gertrude. She, upon approaching the sacrament, expressed the desire to receive it with the same sentiments as the holy virgin and the greatest saints. Then the Saviour appeared to her and told her: 'Now you appear to the citizens of heaven really adorned as you wished to be.'

God looks to the best in you. From the whole biography of a Roman officer the Bible records only a few minutes in which he showed strong faith (Matthew 8:10). Of the whole degraded life of a Samaritan woman, the Bible retains one day when she was a zealous missionary (John 4:30). From everything which you think, if you have the desire to be as holy as man has ever been, God will retain this one inner wish. All your other thoughts will be set aside.

Inwardly formulate the highest wishes even if you do not have the slightest power to fulfill them, and you will receive the highest praise.

Outwardly we can master ourselves only in part. Our strongest decisions are consumed by the fire which we have in our blood. We cannot check the inner movements of our souls while we are awake and we have even less control during sleep.

Have the right desires and do not be afraid. It is written, 'The Lord was with Joseph' (Genesis 39:2). Not everything Joseph did was right. Anyone who knows what despots the ancient kings were cannot imagine Joseph being prime-minister of Egypt without making grave compromises with his conscience. He had to bow before the gods of Egypt, and to conform to the habits of the heathen. But God also knew his moments of victory over temptation. And He knew Joseph's highest desire, which remained valid before Him even if it was unfulfilled in Joseph.

The Lord was with Joseph and will be with you, if

beyond outward deeds and inward thoughts, even if not feeling love, you desire to love. If you desire holiness without having the slightest beginning of it, holiness will be imparted to you.

53: God's thankfulness to you

Cleanse yourself within and God will be thankful to you. God thankful! Such an idea may never have occurred to you, but it is implied in the sermon on the mount: 'For if ye love them which love you, what thank have ye?' (Luke 6:32). Now, thanks from whom? Evidently from God. He thanks you if you can love those who do not love you.

The ear of wheat and the flower bow in gratitude towards the earth from whence came the water and minerals they needed in order to grow. And through Christ's descent to earth, God Himself bowed in thanks to all those like Abraham, Joseph, Moses, Buddha and innumerable others, who overcame human attachments, lust, greed, and selfishness, who loved those unworthy of love, who did good to those who had given them evil, and who lent without hope of receiving.

Jesus bowed gratefully before the apostles who gave up everything for Him, and washed their feet. He knew that all these apostles had tragic lives and dramatic deaths ahead of them because of their love for Him, and so He bowed before them like a servant and washed their feet.

Cultivate good thoughts toward your fellow men. If they have wronged you, remember that all their evil is 'such stuff as dreams are made of.' After a few years, you yourself will not remember it. Evil works die as men die and as dreams vanish. The Bible speaks about 'dead works' (Hebrews 6:1). A man's evil toward you will have passed away but your good thoughts about him will remain. If good thoughts do not arise spontaneously in you, will to have them even though your heart still harbors resentment or hatred. God does not judge the surface of your heart, but looks to your deeper regret that such voices remain inside you.

Take special advantage of the moments immediately after Holy Communion. The King is within you then as surely as He was in the womb of Virgin Mary. This is the time for inner communion with the inner king.

We often act like madmen. When He is outside, surrounding us, we chatter within ourselves; when He is inside, we are busy gossiping outside. Do not fear the ugly voices which speak within you. God knows what to do about them.

The Rabbi of Berditschev once prayed: 'Lord of the Universe, the people of Israel are the phylacteries of thy forehead. When a Jew drops his phylacteries, he lifts them up with loving care, cleanses them of every stain and then, with a kiss, makes amends for their abasement. Lord of the World, They phylacteries are fallen to the ground.'

God is closer to you than you are to yourself; He feels your griefs and your joy more keenly than you do. Your evil thoughts stain His holy name more deeply than your own, so He will be sure to free you of them, to keep you holy in spite of them or even to bring some good out of them.

A mother's love for her child is more tender than the child's self love. Rely on Christ for this too. Think about Him as you would think about a loving mother.

In Hebrew the word for Holy Spirit is a female noun. Catherine of Sienna might not have known Hebrew, but she had the right intuition, for whenever she went to Communion she considered herself as a child sucking the breast of her mother.

Your wrongful inner talks are forgiven even before you utter them. It is only righteous that it should be so. Before we are born, before we have done the slightest evil, we are already sentenced to death because of offenses committed by others. Before the Jewish people existed and could offend God in any way, God told Abraham that his descendents would be enslaved in a foreign country for four centuries (Genesis 15:13). It is only fair that we be forgiven even before repentance, because of what the new Adam did for us on the cross.

You think forgiven evil thoughts, you speak forgiven inner words. You hear inner voices today which in the spiritual reality have long since been erased. Time is a confusion in your mind. You hear today what belongs to your past. Your present is intimate communion with Him.

You can make God rejoice over you with singing (Zephaniah 3:17). Do not miss the opportunity.

54: The Lord of hosts

Theologians speak about the attributes of God. The Bible never mentions such a thing. The very word, 'attributes,' implies qualities which are assigned to Him by men. Hindoo religion rightly distinguishes btween Brahman Nirguna, Godhead as it is, and Brahman Saguna, Godhead as we see it. The Biblical name corresponding to Brahman Nirguna is 'El eljon,' — 'the most high God' (Genesis 14:19).

Touch the wing of a butterfly and you destroy the splendors of its colors. The holy contents of the notion 'Godhead' is desecrated through investigation. The Biblical names of God are equivalent to what Indians call Brahman Saguna and must be accepted with caution. Divine, mysterious existence is encased in the words of a fallen race whose language cannot possibly express the reality of God.

'Lord of hosts' is not one of God's names, but is simply how some men thought of him during a certain period of spiritual evolution.

Once they called him Lord of Hosts, certain conclusions followed. He ordered Joshua to set an ambush for the enemy (Joshua 8:1–2). 'Joshua destroyed all that breathed, as the Lord God of Israel had commanded' (10:40). By the same command, he 'set a city on fire' (8:8). 'Joshua offered burnt offerings unto the Lord,' after having killed all the inhabitants of Ai (8:31) because of such an order.

Calvin believed all these things literally. He wrote, 'The literal sense of Scripture is the whole essence of faith and Christian theology. It is better to confess ignorance than to play with frivolous guesses. Allegories are the scum of the Holy Spirit, they are harlots seducing me.'

I am a disciple of what is called the typological school. I believe that the accounts of the wars in the Bible are symbols of our own spiritual battles.

God sides with no army. Nehemiah says, 'There was no beast with me save the beast that I rode upon' (2:12). We have no enemy except the one within ourselves. The assembling of armies is always a bad sign. Even victorious armies have no real splendor, and to find them glorious implies delight in the slaughter of men. Lao Tsu rightly says that 'victories should be treated as funeral rites.' A man of God exercises quiet restraint and avoids using weapons whenever possible.

The many accounts of war in the Bible are of great value to us in a negative sense.

Indris Shah again tells the sufite story: A man got lost in a forest. He wandered for several days unable to find a way out. Then he met a wild, unkempt-looking man whom he assumed to be an inhabitant of the wood. He asked the man for directions. 'I myself have been lost in this forest for 10 years,' replied the man. — 'Then you cannot help me,' the first said. — 'On the contrary,' said the other. 'I can show you hundreds of paths which do not lead out of the wood.' Negative experiences have exceptional value. The many histories of war in the Bible teach that nothing is achieved by war.

Jesus is the Prince of peace. Seek the ways of peace.

55: What is Abraham's greatness?

Why does Abraham play such a prominent role throughout the Bible? Why are all nations blessed in his seed? Why can no one be saved except through becoming an heir of Abraham and entering into the covenant which God made with him? He was far from always being a good man. Why did God choose him?

God does not choose the best, but those whom he intends to make best.

God's first lesson for Abraham was to be ready, for his faith, to reject his civilization and form a minority of one. The Midrash, (a Rabbinical commentary to the Old Testament) tells us that Abraham's father, Terah, was a builder of idols. As a boy Abraham wished to test them. He prepared food, put it before the biggest idol and waited to see if it would eat. When it did not, he chopped up all the idols with an axe and put the axe in the hand of the largest. When his father returned home, he found the havoc and asked for an explanation. Abraham said, 'I brought food to the gods. They quarrelled over who should have the most, and the big one smashed the heads of the others.' The father replied, 'Don't be silly. These gods cannot move. Tell me what really happened. . .'

Then Abraham said, 'Well, if they cannot move, they are not gods,' and he chopped off the head of the last idol and ran away from home. At first he worshipped the moon, but when he realized it faded before the sun, he adored the sun. But the sun too was transitory, so he came to believe in the one unseen God who had made sun, moon and all other things. When this faith of Abraham's was rejected by all his people, he left them, preferring to be with God, even if alone.

Next God taught Abraham obedience. Although Abraham had treated Hagar and Ishmael harshly, he could also be soft-hearted. When God told him He would destroy Sodom and Gomorrah, he pleaded for them.

When he was commanded to bring his only beloved son, Isaac, as a sacrifice, he did not pray for the son to be spared.

We do not know why God asked for Isaac's sacrifice. Perhaps the son had committed an evil deed worthy of such punishment.

In Romania, an officer was suspect of treason during wartime. His father, a general, asked the king for permission to preside over the military tribunal which would sentence his son to death. Abraham might have had to show that one must sacrifice affection for the sake of morality.

In any case, when God asked Abraham to sacrifice Isaac, he contradicted his own law which forbade killing, as well as his promise to establish an everlasting covenant with Isaac and his seed (Genesis 17:19). Isaac had no children. With his death, everything would be finished. But Abraham, by fulfilling a commandment which contradicted the law and the promise, put God under an obligation to forgive us when we stray from the law or break our own promises.

Although Abraham might not always have been good, there was surely greatness in him.

56: Why is God harsh against some?

Before the settlement of the state of Massachusetts, God wiped out the Indians by plague. Winthrop, who was governor of the state at that time said, 'If we have no right to this land, yet our God has right to it. If he be pleased to give it to us taking it from people who have so long usured upon him and abused his creature, who shall control him on his terms?'

To a modern Christian reader it might seem strange that I wrote, 'God wiped out the Indians by a plague.' Well, if not He, then who? I wrote in Biblical language. Except for what is written in the Bible, we know about the essence of God as much as a fly knows about the nature of a king.

God says, 'I plagued Egypt' (Joshua 24:5). God wiped out the Canaanite nations, women, children and all.

Some ask whether this was ethical, but how ethical is ethics when it judges God? God is sovereign.

If the word 'morality' can be applied to God, He must be said to employ a different morality from ours. A general remains well protected in the rear while he commands his soldiers forward into enemy fire. Is this ethical? A ruler may sentence a citizen to death, although the citizens are forbidden to kill. As social life differs from private life, even less is the behavior of God meant to resemble ours.

At first glance it might seem unreasonable that the One who condemns us for killing even a single person should lawfully destroy whole populations. But all laws are based only on the will of God. He changes them when he likes. They are not necessary in themselves. Reason and faith are two separate conditions which do not harmonize in all things. There are even two separate logics, the physical one and that of faith. Aristotelian

115

logic does not apply to religion in which 1 is equal to 3, one God a trinity.

The life of believers defies ordinary logic. Every believer should hate war, the killing of God's creatures whom we are taught to love; but we also remember, 'Machir . . . was a man of war, therefore he had Ghilead and Bashan' (Joshua 17:1). Though it is important for a believer not to fight, it is also important that Ghilead should be possessed by him and not by people full of hatred. While we must loathe war, we also had to defeat Hitler, the lover of war. The logic of faith solves such problems.

57: Implications of our prayers

The 'Our Father' is given us as a warning against using too many words in prayer. Every request from God has many implications.

When we say, 'Thy kingdom come,' we should not use these words without knowing their consequences.

We say, 'Come, Lord Jesus' (Revelation 22:20) but it is written, 'Let no man deceive you by any means: for that day shall not come except there comes a falling away first,' the great apostasy (II Thessalonians 2:3). Whole nations will forsake the Christian faith: 'The Christians will be hated by all nations for Christ's name sake. And then shall many be offended and shall betray one another' (Matthew 24:1-10). You wish for the Lord's coming. But have you made your decision? Will you be among the traitors or among the betrayed?

The coming of Christ brings eternal, definitive doom

for unbelievers, among whom will be many of your cherished friends. It is written 'Woe unto you that desire the day of the Lord! To what end is it for you? The day of the Lord is darkness and not light' (Amos 5:18).

Do you wish Jesus to come? On that day the believers 'shall go forth and look upon the carcasses of the men who have transgressed against God, for their worm shall not die neither shall their fire be quenched (Isaiah 66:24). Perhaps among these carcasses shall be members of your own family.

The Jews cannot bear to read this as the last verse of Isaiah and in their synagogues, in public readings, they repeat after this verse the comforting one which precedes it. They also do this after the last verse of Malachi which concludes the Old Testament with the words of God: 'Lest I come and smite the earth with a curse.'

But however you read it, the situation will be the same. When the Lord comes, all His opponents shall perish.

Although this wrath is beneficent, although their being consumed will show them that 'God rules in Jacob unto the ends of the earth' (Psalm 59:13), nonetheless it will be a difficult day to bear. Are you prepared to bear it?

The answer depends on whether you are born again. For those who have passed through new birth the sight of hell will be a source of joy. St Thomas Acquinas wrote that the tortures of the damned will be one of the delights of heaven. This is because we will be changed in a manner which we cannot now imagine. 'Eye has not seen, nor ear heard, neither have entered into the heart of man the things that God has prepared for them that love Him' (I Corinthians 2:9).

After a conversion the things which made you happy before become abhorrent and the things which displeased you become your joy. So, in the glorified body, we will appreciate the righteousness and the wrath of God in a manner incomprehensible for us now. Can an alcoholic believe that he will ever come to hate alcohol? So we cannot fathom that we will ever rejoice at seeing hell. It must be enough for us that it seems good in His sight (Matthew 11:26).

It is written that it pleased God to bruise Jesus (Isaiah 53.10). In our present stage of development this is unintelligible. But if God can find pleasure in the innocent suffering of His Son, knowing the purpose it accomplishes, it might easily be that we will find pleasure in the righteous punishment of the wicked.

'Thy kingdom come.' Do not speak these words lightly.

58: The inerrancy of the Bible

Inerrancy of the Bible is an article of faith for Christians. Reason is insufficient to prove it because there is no infallible mind which, having examined all arguments for and against, can establish the Bible's infallibility.

According to Gödel's incompleteness theorem, no system can prove its own consistency without recourse to concepts that the system itself cannot generate but which are supplied from outside by a larger system, subject itself like everything else in this world to incompleteness and so on and so on. You overcome this only through a leap of faith. I belong to the Church established by Christ and it is our faith that the Bible is inerrant.

But which Bible? Not only are there numerous translations, but also there are texts which are included in some scriptures and excluded from others.

There are over 5,000 manuscripts of the New Testament. No two agree. Early copies call the robber pardoned by Pilate 'Jesus Barabbas.' Later copyists found this confusing and offensive and omitted the word 'Jesus' from the robber's name.

Mark 16:9–20 and John 5:3–4 are missing from all old manuscripts, and Mark 11:26 is omitted by almost all.

When the church historian Eusebius died in 340, only a segment of the Church acknowledged the epistles of Jacob, Jude, II and III John, and II Peter as Scripture. Luther never acknowledged the epistle of James, even though he translated it.

St Athanasius, who died in 364, was the first teacher to quote all 27 books of the New Testament.

The Sinaiticus, a text of the New Testament from the third century, includes two letter of Barnabas and a book, 'The pastor Hermas,' which is excluded from our Bibles.

Books which are so inspired that Biblical authors quote them, 'The book of the wars of the Lord' (Numbers 21:14), 'The book of Jasher' (Numbers 10:13), and many others are not included in Scripture.

There is also a vast difference in texts among the manuscripts which exist. Here are four versions of I Corinthians 15:51, all equally correct depending on which Greek manuscript is consulted:

'We shall not all sleep, but we shall all be changed.'

'We shall all sleep, but we shall not all be changed.'

'We shall not all sleep, nor shall we all be changed.'

'We shall all rise, but we shall not all be changed.'

In another familiar passage, only one Greek letter makes the difference between the King James Version's translation, 'Glory to God in the highest, and on earth peace, good will to men,' and the Revised Standard Version's, 'Glory to God in the highest, and on earth peace among men with whom he is well pleased.' Some manuscripts have that letter; some do not. Other Bible verses can be read in over ten different ways.

The discoveries at the Dead Sea of old Biblical manuscripts have complicated the problem even more. The scrolls essentially confirm previous Scriptures, but also differ from them in certain parts.

In the Old Testament, the name Nebuchadnezzar is spelled in seven different ways. Which is the inerrant spelling?

The conclusion to be drawn from this is that God has willed to give us a text with variations, problems, missing parts: a text which should leave our minds perplexed and should be one more factor in convincing us that in faith we do not have to rely on reason.

In Jerusalem there are two places believed to have been Golgotha, and two sepulchres of Jesus. For many other important Biblical events, several sites are claimed. It is because the Biblical events are not merely geographically located: they fill the whole world. Jesus died only once for our salvation. But He is crucified afresh as often as saints fall away (6.6). The church is also the prolongation of His life. In this sense, there are innumerable Golgothas and places where Jesus is buried and where he performs miracles. So it is with the Bible. It is inerrant, but it does not have only one text. Christians have lived and believed and died martyrs' deaths for various texts. The truth of God shines through many texts and through various translations.

59: Problems of punctuation in the Bible

The original manuscripts of the Bible have no punctuation. Sentences without punctuation put our minds to work. The sentence, 'Charles I walked and talked half an hour after his head was cut off' is obviously absurd.

It acquires meaning when commas are placed after 'talked' and before 'his.' We must also sometimes work hard to guess a Biblical writer's intention.

Genesis 22:2, as it stands in the Authorized Version, is incorrect because of wrong punctuation. We read 'Take now thy son, thine only son Isaac, whom thou lovest.' But Isaac was not Abraham's only son. If the last comma is omitted, the passage makes sense: 'thine only son Isaac whom thou lovest.' Ishmael had not been loved.

Luke 23:43 is punctuated in a certain way by Seventh Day Adventists and others who do not believe in immediate entrance into eternal life after death, but think that the dead remain dead until a resurrection on the final day. They read, 'Verily I say unto thee today, thou shalt be with me in paradise.' The mainstream of Christianity prefers the following punctuation: 'Verily I say unto thee, today thou shalt be with me in paradise.' Paradise can be entered immediately after death, provided one had faith in the Lord.

Much depends upon punctuation in John 14:6 also. As it now reads in the Authorized Version, Jesus says He is three things: the way, the truth and the life. I personally do not understand what being the way means. A primitive in the Philippines, when told by a missionary that Jesus is the way, asked, 'What kind of a way? Is it a mountain trail?'

My punctuation would be: 'I am the way: the truth and the life.' Truth has absolute demands which, if fulfilled, would annihilate life. Life has desires which can be totally fulfilled only through renouncing the truth. He who has come not only full of truth, because mankind could not bear the truth alone, but full of 'grace *and* truth' (John 1:17), showed the way again on the last evening. The way is a loving attention to the demands of both, of life and truth.

Romans 9:5 can be punctuated in at least three ways, giving three different meanings:

(1) 'Christ came, who is over all God. . .' This is the

only text in which Paul declares Christ to be God. The verse was thus understood by the majority of interpreters until the 8th century.

(2) 'Christ came, God who is over all be blessed for ever.' So Erasmus. It is a doxology to God, not an assertion that Christ is God.

(3) 'Christ came, who is over all, God be blessed for ever.' Here the praise is divided between Christ and God.

Let us thank God for the diversity of thoughts which are given through the Scriptures. Everything is possible to God, including all the different punctuations and translations of the Bible which express His truth.

60: Does the Bible teach literalism?

Due respect must be given to every letter of the Bible, but the Bible has been written with a purpose: to bring men to salvation. Therefore its authors sometimes sacrifice the letter. The purpose is more important than the means.

Paul quotes Hosea as having said, 'I will call them my people which were not my people, and her beloved, which was not beloved. And it shall come to pass that in the place where it was said unto them, Ye are not my people, there shall they be called the children of the living God' (Romans 9:25–26). The translation is not literal and does not correspond to any version of the Hebrew text. Paul felt free to adapt the text for his own purpose. He applied to the Gentiles words which were intended by the Jewish prophet for the ten tribes of

Israel separated from Judah (Hosea 1:4–2:23) and made them sound more forceful.

In Romans 11:26, Paul gives the great teaching, 'All Israel shall be saved.' Needing some verses from the Old Testament to substantiate the promise, he says, 'It is written: There shall come out of Sion the deliverer.' But these words are not to be found anywhere. In Psalm 14:7, David had expressed a desire, 'Oh that the salvation of Israel were come out of Sion.' Certain that God has fulfilled this pious desire, Paul modifies David's words so that they no longer express a wish but an assurance: 'The deliverer shall come out of Sion.'

Paul assures the Jewish believers, 'The deliverer shall turn away ungodliness from Jacob' (Romans 11:26), saying that this too is written. The only possible reference is to Isaiah 59:20 where no such promise is given. There we read that the Redeemer shall come unto them that turn from transgression. It is Jacob who has to turn away from sin, not the Deliverer who will cause the turning. But Paul, when he read Isaiah, realized that men cannot change their hearts through their own endeavors. This must be the work of the Lord. He quotes the verse according to his own interpretation and not literally, as it is in the Old Testament.

We should also remember that many of Paul's epistles were written in prisons where he had to quote from memory, not having the scrolls of the Old Testament at hand.

Matthew quotes in his Gospel 2:23 'what was spoken by the prophets' about Jesus: 'He shall be called a Nazarene.' However these words cannot be found in any prophetical book. The worse for them. They should have been there. Matthew renders the prophets the favor of putting these words in their mouths. It is like attributing some words of John Chrysostom to a poor preacher whom you wish to uplift.

The sons of Jacob are enumerated in the Bible in 17 different sequences, showing the unimportance of sequences in the timeless sphere to which belief in the Bible moves us.

Value every letter of the Bible but seek fulfillment of the aim which is beyond it: the salvation of souls. Do not be like the child in Khartoum who loved the statue of General Gordon riding on a camel. Every day the lad asked to be taken to see General Gordon. When he reached the age of seven he asked, 'Who is the uncle riding on General Gordon?' He had mistaken the camel for the hero. The Bible is not God: it is the carrier of His message.

61: About angels

It is normal for a Christian to commune with angels. The Lord has said, 'Ye shall see heaven open and the angels of God ascending and descending' (John 1:51).

This is not a privilege reserved only for children of God, but for all men of prayer. Cornelius, a heathen, 'saw an angel of God coming in to him' (Acts 10:3). When he told the story to Peter, he did not express any amazement (Acts 10:30). Why else do angels exist if not to serve men? An angel of the Lord also came to Peter himself (Acts 12:7).

The gap between man and angel is not so big as we imagine. Men are the tadpoles of angels. Angels are accomplished believers. The Lord has said that in the resurrection we will be like the angels of God in heaven (Matthew 22:30), implying that now we are embryonic angels, sure to attain full growth, because fortunately abortions are unknown in the spheres above.

Why do we not all see angels?

Their appearance can be dangerous for those who are spiritually unprepared, a shock, like touching a high-power electrical wire. The keepers of Jesus' tomb 'became as dead' when they saw the angel of the Lord (Matthew 28:4). So angels sometimes present themselves garbed as men. Cornelius tells Peter, 'A man stood before me in bright clothing.' On the ascension day, the apostles beheld 'two men in white apparel' (Acts 1:10). They were angels.

You cannot be sure that you have not met an angel. Perhaps you did not recognize him as such. The Bible recommends hospitality. 'Thereby some have entertained angels unaware' (Hebrews 13:1).

Keep communion with angels. Value them, but at the same time know their limitations. They do not know everything. Each angel has only a certain assignment and can do no more.

If the angel who announced to the virgin that she would become pregnant with the Lord had also told Joseph, there would have been one sadness less. But he could not — he had received only one commission.

If the angel who warned Joseph of the danger to the life of the infant Jesus had also told all parents in Bethlehem about Herod's evil intentions, a mass slaughter would have been avoided. But the angel did not know everything.

Seek therefore communion with the Lord Himself.

For mysterious purposes of their own, angels sometimes fight with men. Do not be afraid. Jacob defeated an angel (Genesis 32:24–28). This is what prevailing prayer is about.

Even if an angel opposes you, you can win. Only One is almighty. Always submit unconditionally to Him alone.

62: When Jesus can't

'Christ Jesus . . . made himself in the likeness of man' (Philippians 2:5–6). He became the most perfect man, but still a man, a being with essential limitations. Certain things he could do; others not.

'In his own country . . . Jesus could do no mighty work' (Mark 6:1–5). He had met unbelief. He had brothers and sisters (Matthew 13:55–56), but they did not believe in him (John 7:5), and Jesus was not able to bring them to conversion. What an education Mary must have given them; but in vain.

It is usually said that the Lord performed 'many' miracles. Blind men received their sight, lame walked, lepers were cleansed, deaf heard, and dead were raised up (Matthew 11:5). But how many?

A dozen may have been awakened from death, but thousands remained dead and their relatives remained uncomforted. Thousands of sick retained their maladies. He fed hungry multitudes on a few occasions, but He did not solve the problem of hunger, not even in little Palestine. Many went to bed without having eaten. Nor could Jesus make all who heard him preach the Gospel accept it.

All Jesus' mighty works happen on a small scale.

This is because he had become human. You too are human. Why then do you wonder, why do you despair about the many things you cannot do?

'Ye cannot do the things that you would' (Galatians 5:17); you cannot fully overcome the lust of your own flesh. You cannot overcome all adverse circumstances. This state is a characteristic feature of human nature. Angels are also limited. Only with God is everything possible.

If you are converted, God helps you to become a saint, but a human saint, who will bring goodness and love into the world of wickedness as the gulf stream brings warmth to the ocean. But the gulfstream is constituted of water, like the cold ocean surrounding it, and its warmth can penetrate only to a certain distance, no more.

The devil wins through spectacular feats. A man in the country of the Gadarenes who was possessed of devils could pluck chains asunder and break fetters in pieces (Mark 5:4). When Jesus drove the demons from him the man became a disciple. He might later have been thrown in jail for his faith, and worn chains for Jesus, as so many thousands have done throughout history. But he could no longer break the fetters. No instance of a chained Christian accomplishing such feats is known.

The Lord does not raise us above the human, but makes us saints in our human weakness. Accept your weakness and bring to it the warmth of love.

63: Before we call, He answers

God says that He will create new heavens and a new earth (Isaiah 65:17). One of the characteristics of life in these is that before their inhabitants call, He will answer (v. 24).

Modern physicists have considered the possibility of an anti-telephone, a device by which the inquirer of the future will get his reply before ringing up to ask the question. What is a theoretical technical development of the future was promised in its fullness to God's children in an age when such technology was not yet dreamed of.

Einstein's special theory of relativity showed that anything traveling at a speed greater than light — which he considered impossible — would go backward in time. Scientists now assert that tachyons, faster-than-light particles are known to exist although they have not yet been detected. Once man is able to handle them, mankind will be caught in a paradox. It will technically be possible to communicate so that answers precede questions, which would mean the cessation of communication.

Perceiving all solutions in advance, problems will stop arising in my mind.

The child who said that Mona Lisa smiled so beautifully because she had an intuition that da Vinci would paint her, and that da Vinci painted her because she smiled exactly as he wished a model to do, was not mistaken.

The spirit passes light in speed. In exceptional circumstances, a man can perceive in the unconscious of a fellow man questions which have not yet arisen to a conscious level, and reply to them. The one who receives the answer does not even know that it is an answer.

Some believers are sad that they do not feel any fellowship with God. But it is not necessary. The communion is established on a faster-than-light level, and consists in God's granting you things for which you never felt any desire. Many believers testify that they have received salvation or other gifts of God for which they have not sought. The wish was in the depth of the soul and was fulfilled before they became aware of it.

Such will be the rule in the new heavens and on the new earth. Communion with God as between two beings who need to communicate will be replaced by union in love. We will be *in* God. Eternity will be an embrace in love. No wind blows any more. We no longer cry out for fear of the tempests, and the tempests no longer need be stilled. Answers precede requests, which therefore are not made. All will be calm, all serene. This is eternity.

64: The body language of Jesus

Besides spoken language, every man has another, the language of the body, which is in fact more ancient than speech. Whoever can understand this language has a deeper insight into his fellow men. See how many gestures of the Lord are reported in the Gospel: the stretching out of his hand, the lifting of the eyes, the touching of children. His body spoke: could it have been less than eloquent? Was it not the word become flesh?

The pupils of the eyes enlarge when something exciting occurs. An honest man looks straight into another's face. A facial tic or the manner of shaking hands speaks volumes. Warm hands or pale, cold ones, specially those with a little black shadow on the central parts, tell much about a man's character. So does a full, straight, smooth and shining face as compared to a crooked or gloomy one.

Body parts too are character clues. Socially active girls are found among those with slender legs rather than among those with big hips.

Jesus would have been completely unintelligible to his disciples had he not had a very developed body language.

He tells them, 'I am come to send fire on earth and what else will I than it should be already kindled?' (Luke 12:49). Any arsonist might have said the same.

When the Salvation Army started its work in India, the governor of Bombay forbade the display of its flag because its motto, 'Blood and fire,' was misleading. Such inflamatory words as Christ's, coming direction from the mouth of a man accused of spreading riot among an oppressed people, could be even more misleading.

Under ordinary circumstances, every peace-loving citizen would have abandoned Him when he proclaimed the kindling of fire as his program, since He did not qualify his words or explain that He meant them symbolically or spiritually. But his eyes, his face, his gestures must have spoken. None of his disciples was disturbed when he spoke such dangerous words, or even when he added, 'Suppose ye that I am come to give peace on earth? I tell you, nay, but rather division' (v. 51).

Two disciples of John the Baptist, looking upon the manner in which Jesus walked, said, 'Behold the lamb of God' (John 1:36). It is written about the Jewish king Ahab that he repented 'and walked softly' (I Kings 21:27). Once I became suspicious that a man was a Soviet infiltrator because of the way he walked. Ensuing events showed that I was probably correct. Jesus walked in a manner apart.

Besides His body language, the intonation of his voice must have been significant. I have already written that the Hebrew Old Testament contains musical notation for every saying and is meant to be chanted rather than recited.

If anyone, even God, had told me as he told Abraham, 'Take your only son whom you love and bring him for a burnt-offering' (Genesis 22:2), I would not have done it. Neither would Abraham. We do not know in what manner God uttered this command. But listen to the words being chanted with transcendent harmonies in a synagogue according to a melody of thousands of years! Abraham, listening, felt peace in his heart and understood it to be only a test, a ritual showing to what length love of God must go, a foreshadowing of God's sacrifice for us. Therefore Abraham immediately fulfilled what was demanded.

We receive guidance from the Lord. Be attentive to its music and to the gestures of the messengers.

65: The numbers and the story

Ancient Hebrew and Greek had no written symbols for figures. Letters were used to express numbers. Every word of Scripture can be understood as part of a story or teaching, or it can be considered as a number because it is constituted of letters which are also figures. The sum of the numerical values of the letters in a word gives its mathematical value.

The first word of the Old Testament, *Bereshit* ('In the beginning') has the numerical value 914:

$$\text{B} \quad \text{r} \quad \text{a} \quad \text{sh} \quad \text{j} \quad \text{t}$$
$$2 + 200 + 1 + 300 + 10 + 400 = 914$$

All Biblical words can be thus transcribed.

The Bible can be a communication in numbers or in text or both. Which is the primary value of the Bible?

Mankind uses thousands of languages and dialects. French- and English-speaking Canadians, French- and Flemish-speaking Belgians, Afrikaansk- and English-speaking South Africans — all engage in bitter conflicts over which language should be spoken in their countries. But all nations of all continents employ the same system of numerals. No disagreement here.

Numbers probably correspond to a deeper layer of the human psyche. Symbols might have been used as figures before they were used as letters.

In 1965, at the site of the New York World's Fair a capsule was buried to be opened after 5,000 years. It contains a message of 1,271 figures containing in mathematical formulae the essential information about life on earth. If in that future time the same symbols are used, like in the Bible, for both letters and figures, those who read the formulae could encounter double meaning, just as we do when reading Scriptures in the original.

The key figure in the Bible is the figure 7, the symbol of human holiness. There are 6 directions in which a man can move: forward, backward, upward, down, to the right or to the left. And there exists something more excellent, the holy attitude, to remain quietly at the center, like Mary Magdalene when she sat still at the feet of Jesus. This is symbolized by 7.

Seven plays an exceptional role in physical reality too. Think of the 7 colors of the rainbow and the 7 musical notes on the diatonic scale.

Two Israeli scientists, Nobel prize winner Isidor Rabi and William Markowitz, discovered 'chordmater universal time,' a system of defining time which is more exact than astronomical measurement. A second is no longer defined as a fraction of the time in which the earth accomplishes an orbit, but is the time which an electron near the outer edge of an atom of cesium wobbles: 9,192,631,770 times. This figure is a multiple of the sacred 7 which is the mathematical seal of God's creation.

The old Semitic people did not have a decimal system, but a heximal one — six figures plus zero. This system passed into Europe through the Arabs and its remnant survives still in the French language which has no words for seventy, eighty, or ninety. These numbers are expressed as sixty-and-ten, four-times-twenty and four-times-twenty-plus-ten.

Since 6 was the last simple figure in the Semitic system, our 7 was written by them as 10, 8 was 11 and so on, until they jumped from 16 to 20. In this system, 10 (our 7) was the first composite figure. It became the symbol for how great a zero, a man of nothing, could become if he placed before himself the great One, God. Therefore 7 is the figure of holiness, and 6, being the last simple figure, became the symbol of pettiness. The apocalyptic beast is 666, the superlative of 6, a paper tiger (Revelation 13:18). Do not fear it. Jesus will destroy it with His breath. The numerical value of Jesus in Greek is 888, the antithesis of 666, surpassing the apogee of human holiness. He represents divine sainthood.

There are secrets enshrined in the mathematical structure of the Bible. We read in Proverbs 1:1, 'Solomon, son of David, king of Israel.' The value of the three proper names is

Solomon	David	Israel	
373	14	541	= 928

which, strangely, is the total number of instructions contained in the whole book of Proverbs. It is like an indication for the reader, 'Seek sense not only in the text of the Bible, but also in its mathematical form.'

The Apostles, all fishermen, toiled a whole night and caught nothing. When the resurrected Lord appeared (John 21) and told them where to throw the nets, they caught many fish. The catch was not due to their skill. Every fish caught was a sign of grace. They counted them and found 153 fish. Is it a simple coincidence that the word 'grace' occurs 153 times in the New Testament?

Every figure in the Bible has a deep meaning. Nothing in it is superfluous.

66: Why so many Biblical questions unanswered?

Having read the Bible, there are a few things we know. Many more questions remain unanswered.

How is it that there is a God? Who made him? Why did He make man? Why did he allow or ordain him to sin? Why does suffering exist? Why do even fish in the depths of the sea have cancer? Why do beings live on each other? Will we know one another in the life hereafter? How is it that the death of a being 2,000 years ago affects the state of our souls? Why is it important that Fiji Islanders should know the stories of the Jewish kings? Why should some souls suffer eternally in hell for sins committed here during only a fragment of time? And so on and so on.

There is a Mexican story which contains the best solution to the problem of all those unanswered questions.

A dwarf named Tchuda, tired of the world's mockery and derision, decided to end his life by throwing himself into the abyss from the mountain Tchumanda. On his way he met the beautiful Armida who was going to commit suicide because of betrayal by her lover. They were joined by prince Christopher who was on order from the King to seek and kill the bandit Fukinama. This thief would be recognized by the six fingers on his right hand.

The three stopped to rest at an old monastery where they were received by the abbot Timothy. Although Timothy had not been a monk for long, the fame of his holiness had already spread far and wide. When Armida bowed to kiss the holy man's hand, she noticed six fingers. The wanted criminal had become a saint.

And. . .

Most people want to know what happened next with the dwarf, the princess, the knight and the king who had ordered the bandit's death. There are some however who do not ask any more questions but are in ecstasy about this one great wonder: the bandit has become a luminous example of love, and when asked how it occurred, he answered, 'God performed it through the sacrifice of Christ.'

The other questions remain unanswered, forgotten. The elect do not ask them anymore. The Bible contains no answers to satisfy the curious.

I hope you are not among these.

67: The forbidding of quarrel

We can discover the facts of nature, we can establish causal relations. We know why certain phenomena will produce others of a predictable nature. We do not know why existence exists, why it is as it is, why there are causal relations and why the effects are these and not others.

One of the basic facts of nature is the struggle for life, a struggle that every living creature has to accept. Every species fights against some other species. The herbivores destroy the life of plants. As for mankind, beginning with the first generation born after the expulsion from paradise, there have always been conflicts, fights, killings.

There is one exception to this rule which God establishes for his children: that even the slightest quarrel must be completely excluded. When elephants fight, the grass is injured, and when Christians attack each other, their souls are doomed for eternity.

The motive of a quarrel is unimportant. An admiral once said to some officers who were clashing, 'I know not what the argument is, but I do know that the enemy is out there.' — 'Christians wrestle not against flesh and blood, but against principalities, against powers, against the rulers of the darkness of this world, against spiritual wickedness in high places' (Ephesians 6:12). Internecine conflict for any reason is not permitted.

With a Christian, harsh criticism addressed against him does not produce a backlash. If you must justify your comportment, you can spend your life trying to satisfy your adversary, instead of taking the actions you have chosen.

Every believer who quarrels with another is foolish and forfeits one of the qualities which characterize him as a believer.

During the reign of Henry VIII, Bishop Ridley and Bishop Cranmer, reformers of the Church in Britain, were so opposed to Bishop Hooper, another eminent reformer, that they put him in prison. They found him guilty of ideas about reformation that were too extreme — he refused the invocation of saints in giving an oath, and disapproved of bishops wearing heavily ornamented vestments. A few years later, under Mary Stuart, all three were imprisoned and finally burned at the stake. From his prison cell, Ridley wrote a conciliatory letter to Hooper.

The wise Indian King Asoka, who took the ideas of his country into Asia Minor and influenced the Essenes, cut into rock the motto: 'samavaya eva sadhuh' — 'Concord alone is meritorious.'

Struggle for life is the general law of nature, but for saints there exists an exemption. They do not struggle for life, but live to combat struggling.

However a limit to concord does exist. A Jewish ballad tells of a little sardine swimming off the shores of Eilat. He meets a shark, and of course politely says 'Shalom' (Peace). One thing leads to another, and to placate the shark, the sardine gives up his tail, some fins from his belly, some scales from his back but nothing helps. In desperation the sardine tells his foe that for a real and lasting peace he is prepared to give everything. Hearing this, the shark relents, utters the magic word 'peace,' bares his teeth and swallows the sardine whole.

There must be a limit to the desire for peace.

Kissinger reportedly said, 'I have gone to the Soviets as the first Christian entered the arena to be devoured by wild beasts, but I was determined to speak to the lion. When I happily exclaimed, "You see, we have agreed to communicate," the lion replied, "I don't know about your side, but what I have to say is simply the grace before a meal." '

Do not quarrel, but do not allow anybody to swallow you either. Children of God are too valuable a species: we have to survive.

68: The truth is only in the whole

There is no single Bible verse on which one can rely absolutely. Only the whole Bible gives the truth. A kidney removed from the body is no longer a kidney, but a piece of meat. Even the commandments given directly by God have meaning only when connected with other parts of Scripture, and augmented by common sense.

Considered alone, the commandment given on Mount Sinai, 'Thou shalt not kill' (Exodus 20:13), is unpracticable. Taken literally it forbids all killing, including the killing of animals. It has to be modified by the idea contained in Genesis 9:3: 'Every moving thing that lives shall be meat for you,' for God has given to some animals other animals as food. The prohibition 'Do not kill' does not forbid hunting for livelihood, which can be considered, as Aristotle put it, 'a just war.'

The Commandment also does not forbid killing in just wars for the defense of the motherland, or in defending an innocent person from attack.

Killing is not forbidden absolutely. Augustine taught that God forbid men to kill without Himself renouncing that right. God says, 'I kill and I make alive,' and indeed, the sixth commandment is given by the same God who orders the death sentence many times. On earth the state authority represents God in this: 'The ruler is the minister of God, a revenger to execute wrath upon him that does evil' (Romans 13:4).

Suicide is killing, even though the murderer is the person killed, and is considered unlawful. But even here there are exceptions. Samson killed himself in order to kill a multitude of God's enemies with him. Christian virgins, preferring purity to life, killed themselves when compelled to become prostitutes under the Roman emperors. Many believers, when they were unable to bear any more torture, committed suicide in Communist and Nazi prisons to avoid becoming traitors.

On the other hand, the interdiction also includes the propagation of hatred. Streicher, the editor of a powerful anti-Jewish magazine in Nazi Germany defended himself at the trial of war criminals in Nuremberg saying that he never even slapped a Jew. Nonetheless he was justly sentenced to death because his publications portrayed the Jews as so disgusting and dangerous that those who read them became possessed by the desire to kill Jews.

Never stop at the letter of isolated verses, but draw all the conclusions they imply.

69: How old is the New Testament?

The New Testament is the more reliable the earlier the texts were recorded. With the passing of time, memories fail and subsequent events make men record things as happening other than as they really did.

Are the Gospels late forgeries as some assert? Intelligent forgers, in order to accredit a book with being old, would specially mention things to make it appear so. There is no sign of this in the New Testament. On the contrary, the Gospels contain certain sayings of Jesus which do not square with future events, and which a later writer would surely have modified to prove the teacher's infallibility.

In Matthew 24:15–16, Jesus tells his disciples in Judaea to flee into the mountains, obviously the mountains of Judaea, when they see Jerusalem besieged. However the church historian Eusebius informs us that the disciples fled instead to Pella, on the East side of the Jordan. A late author of the Gospel would have modified Jesus' speech in such a way that their departure to such a distance and, as consequence, their break with Judaism, was foretold or ordered by Jesus.

According to Luke 21:20, Jerusalem would be encircled by armies. This took place during the fall of Judaea to the Babylonians, not during the Roman siege. But Jesus was not speaking in military terms. A city attacked by an overpowering army can be said to be encompassed by horror. A later author would have made an exact description of the many sufferings which were to befall the Jewish nation at that time. He would not have missed magnifying Jesus' prophetic rôle by knowing every detail in advance. However our only knowledge of the atrocities comes from the historian Jesephus Flavius.

In Egypt a papyrus was discovered showing that John's Gospel circulated in Egypt at the end of the first century. The Gospel must have been written before 70 A.D. because it does not mention the destruction of the temple of Jerusalem which occurred at that time. The temple is there described as functioning, and when Jesus speaks of destroying it, the Jews tell Him, 'Forty and six years was this temple in building' (John 2:20). . . Even the Acts of the Apostles must have been written before the destruction of the temple. Had they been written later, this event would have been used to show what a great prophet Jesus had been: He had predicted the destruction of the temple and, behold, it happened.

The five porches of the pool mentioned in John 5:2 were buried under rubble at the fall of Jerusalem. So they remained until excavated recently. The Gospel says *There is* at Jerusalem a pool, having five porches.'

The devil has tried everything to dispel belief in the Bible. A scholar, who might be sincere and not know for whom he works, could point out that what is called the 1st epistle of John has 39 Greek expressions which do not appear in John's Gospel, whereas the Gospel uses thirty words not found in the epistle, etc. Linguistic

139

specialists analyzing my own writings of different periods, books written before and after my imprisonment, would likewise conclude that they are not from the same author.

Those who doubt the authenticity of the authorship of the New Testament would do well to doubt their doubts. We can rely on the Gospels. They were surely written very early by first-hand witnesses.

70: No history book

There are those who debate whether or not the Bible is a reliable history book. It is a phantom question. The Bible is no history book at all. The word 'history' occurs nowhere in it. The word which comes closest is the Hebrew, *toldot*, but this is used only to indicate genealogy or origin.

Biblical personalities are much interested in the past. Joshua wishes to speak to the Jewish people about an immediate question, but begins by enumerating the important events which took place 400 years earlier (Chapter 24). When Stephen, the first martyr of Christianity, is charged with blasphemy, instead of speaking in his own defense, he tells the lives of all the forefathers beginning with Abraham (Acts 7).

But the Biblical manner of recounting the past does not constitute what modern men regard as history. The succeeding generations are spoken of not as about men of different times, but as all one. Joshua says, 'Your eyes have seen what I have done in Egypt' (24:6). Those who had actually seen God's miracles in Egypt had died in the desert, and Joshua spoke now to a new generation which had never been in Egypt. Still he says, '*Your* eyes have seen,' not, 'the eyes of your parents.'

Jesus says to his apostles, 'Ye shall be witnesses unto me . . . unto the uttermost part of the earth' (Acts 1:8). The apostles however, did not even know about the extremities of the earth. But it is their teaching and example and spirit which witnesses even now on all continents, after 2,000 years. Jesus makes no distinction between the first apostles and their successors after many generations.

The Biblical story cannot be called history, because it mocks objectivity. It pursues an aim, and things are told in a manner conducive for attaining it.

In the books of Chronicles there are 323 verses regarding the arrangement of the temple cult, 73 on David's activities and 100 on Judah's genealogy. The Messiah had to come from this tribe and what happened in the temple was more important than the king's politics.

In II Chronicles, 480 verses deal with the very few pious kings and only 342 with the 17 wicked ones. The rulers of the dissident Samaria are omitted completely. Edifying episodes are heightened. The result is more an ideal picture than a real one.

The Jewish writings record the convictions of the writers more than the facts.

The author of Chronicles was probably a Levite. In his books, the Levites are mentioned 100 times, whereas in the books of Kings they are mentioned only once and in those of Samuel, only twice.

In I Chronicle 1–9, all narrative is eliminated. What is important religiously is the transmission of the seed of David from which the Messiah will stem. Therefore in the beginning of the IInd book of Chronicles there are 102 verses about the descendants of Judah, 81 about those of Levi and only 186 about those from the other 10 tribes.

'But one thing is needful' (Luke 10:42). Do not pursue 'objectivity', but rather make your memory and your history serve this one thing, the triumph of the Word of God.

71: Our attitude toward rulers

Every Christian could take as his motto Shakespeare's words, 'May that thought when I imagine ill against my king and brethren be my last breathing in this mortal world.'

Such loyalty from a citizen puts an obligation on the ruler. Among the Jews, the chosen people, 'the king's palace was by the court of the prison' (Nehemiah 3:25). This is the right place for a king to dwell — where he can always have in view how much his sovereignty costs those over whom he rules.

In order for the king to have the majesty and the power of a ruler, others must die in wars under his command. Orphans remain behind. Driven by poverty and lack of education, they end in prison. The king may have neglected to spread morality among his people. His life should remain close to the lowliest of the rejected so he will perceive his kingdom truly.

In Biblical Greek, 'to rule' and 'to feed' is the same word, *poimaino*. What matters is not how many state banquets the king attends, but how much care he has taken that the hungry be fed.

In Aramaean the name for Jesus, 'lamb of God' is *talya Aeloha*, which also means 'servant of God.' The king can be the first servant of a country only if he has the character of a lamb.

Unfortunately not all Jewish kings had this character. Solomon, although his might as a religious poet is undenied, as king, is remembered for two things: his many wives and concubines and his love of luxury. The heathen king Hamurabi is known in history for his righteous laws; likewise the Indian king, Asoka. But not Solomon.

How did he administrate his country? What was his economic policy? What were the relationships between the different classes of the population? Did he provide for charity? Were his judgments righteous or abusive?

His son, Rehoboam, said to the people about Solomon that his father loaded them with a heavy 'yoke' and chastised them with 'whips' (1 Kings 12.2). When you read about the Roman Caesars, some French and English kings, Hitler, Stalin, a shudder passes through you. Good rulers have always been the rare exception.

If the ruler does not fulfill his duty, the believing citizen has to review his attitude. Every nation has a ruler, but also an angel (Daniel 10:13). The angel can be in conflict with the civilian authority. Then the believer must obey the highest authority, the angel.

Let us remember that Elijah resisted arrest (II Kings 1:10), bringing death upon the officers of an unrighteous king.

The Christian is a loyal citizen of a country, but not a bootlicker of tyrants.

72: Commanded love

One of God's strangest commandments is that we should love him (Deuteronomy 6:5). Can love be commanded? Can a young man command a girl, 'Love me and not somebody else?' Could she do this through her own effort?

The imperative 'Love' can be expressed in Hebrew in two forms: *Ohev* can mean only the order to love. *Ahavta* has a double sense, both the imperative 'love' and the perfect tense of the verb: 'You have loved.' *Ahavta* is used by the Bible in this text, not *Ohev*.' Thus God reminds you, 'You come from Me; I shaped your soul;

143

you loved me once; I was your great passion. This was your first sentiment although you may have forgotten it; but now remember, *Ahavta*, you loved me once. Return to this first love!' This is the deep sense of the Biblical commandment. It is the only perspective from which God can be loved with the entire heart.

From the earthly point of view, love of God contains a dose of foolishness. I owe Him gratitude for many blessings, and I admire many of His creations. But why did He create the deadly scorpions and the virusses of so many illnesses? Why are there earthquakes and floods and bereavements? Why so much poverty and injustice in a world in which He is almighty? Why is Christianity such a small light? Why do hundreds of millions live and die in darkness? Could the punishment of sinners not be less than an eternal hell?

The fact that my thoughts are not conjoined with His shows that I have no imaginary God. If I had decided how God should be, I would have chosen Him to create a universe without suffering, age and death. But I know I have the real God because my heart, the heart of a fallen sinner, is in disagreement with Him.

God said to Adam, 'Of the tree of knowledge of good *and* evil, thou shalt not eat' (Genesis 2:17). Man has to choose between good and evil, one or the other — he cannot have them both. God is otherwise, as are those in the heavenly spheres. They know both good *and* evil (Genesis 3:22). This is the cleavage between us.

The ultimate good is unintelligible for us, so we cannot be commanded, 'Love God.' Instead we must be reminded that we come from the sphere where things are known otherwise. The Lord says, 'Return.' Remember, *Ahavta*, you *have loved*. Return to your first love. Seated in heavenly spheres, the veil will be lifted and you will receive new understanding.

There you will understand an ancient mystical teaching which has never been written, but is expressed in a Japanese dance. Once there was a prince of such beauty that all who beheld him could do nothing else. All activity ceased in his presence. So the prince donned an ugly mask in order for men to live. Perhaps you can understand from this the existence of a beneficent God and yet of so much suffering.

Let us love God as He is known in heaven to deserve. Bernard of Clairvaux said, 'The measure of loving God is to love Him without measure.' Do not love Him for His special gifts — at a certain moment he may withhold them. Love Him without reason. Sometimes He may afflict you. When Israel was young, he loved God and followed Him in the wilderness (Jeremiah 2:2). Love Him like this again.

73: Peculiarities of the Hebrew alphabet

When the Japanese Imperial orchestra plays their own national music, they have no conductor. Harmony is achieved because the musicians breathe in the same rhythm, constituting, as it were, a single organism. This is how we can understand why Jesus breathed the Holy Spirit upon his apostles.

You sense something of this when you read the Bible. Dozens of authors have contributed to it, with no single coordinator to harmonize the writings. But the authors breathed the same air of heavenly spheres in the same rhythm.

The Hebrew alphabet teaches you not so much how to read and write, but how to breathe. Two letters, the *aleph* and the *ayin* are unsounded. In transliteration the former is represented by the smooth breathing sign 'é' and the latter by that of rough breathing, 'è'. When these letters are pronounced, you hear nothing: the speaker opens and closes his mouth without making the slightest sound. Jesus said to John, 'I am the Alpha and the Omega' (Revelation 1:8). These are two letters of the Greek alphabet. But Jesus and John were both Jewish and it is unlikely that they would have spoken with one another in Greek. Jesus must have spoken Hebrew. Might he not have said, 'I am the Aleph and the Ayin, which would mean, 'I am the silence and the even deeper silence'? Or will He have said "I am the Aleph and the Tav, the last letter of the Hebrew alphabet, which was written at that time +, a cross? Will the sense have been "I am the silence and the cross"?

The *Yod* is often silent. My beloved is mine' says the bride in the song, '*Dodi li*.' In the word *li*, which stands for 'mine,' the *yod* is silent, one might even say quiescent, giving peace. No need even to pronounce it. She continues, *veani lo* (Song 2:16) and 'I am his.' *Lo*, the word for 'his' ends with the letter *vav*, again unsounded, quiescent. What long speeches Romeo and Juliet deliver to each other. Not so here. The mutual possession is so sure and so strong that words cease.

Just as the Hebrew alphabet starts with a silent letter, the Bible is more conspicuous by its silences than by its words. It is silent about the first thirty years of Jesus' life. We know that at the age of 12 Jesus spoke with the priests in the temple but the subjects they discussed are not revealed. Magdalene sat a whole night at Jesus' feet and listened to him, but we are not told what He said.

In many places in the Hebrew Bible, the sign ⌐ called *Athnach* (respiration) divides verses into two main clauses, as for example, in Psalm 2:1, 'Why do the people rage (respiration) and the people imagine a vain thing?' Omission of a deep respiration in the midst of this verse would result in a reading unfaithful to the Hebrew text. Other readers breathe at the same point and this establishes the harmony of the orchestra.

There are many words in the Bible whose aim is to bring you to the great silence. 'The Lord is in his holy

74: Orthographical errors in the Bible

The renowned American preacher Billy Sunday once said, 'If the English language gets in my way, I tramp all over it.' This is the sentiment of the Biblical authors too.

There are a few letters of the Hebrew alphabet which are written one way when they occur at the beginning or middle of a word, but which have another form when used at the end.

This rule of orthography is unfailingly respected throughout the Bible with but one exception. A strange 'orthographic error' has been perpetuated for 3,000 years in all Hebrew manuscripts and printed Bibles, and never corrected. The synagogue keeps the error in the Bible even though few of the rabbis could provide an explanation.

In Isaiah 9:6–7, some 700 years before the birth of Christ, the coming of a child who will be the prince of peace is announced. 'Of the increase of his government and peace there shall be no end.' The Hebrew expression for 'of the increase' is *lemarbeh*, written with a final 'm' in the midst of the word.

The Kabbalah, a collection of old Jewish writings containing mystical thoughts explains that the coming of this child was prophesied in the Scripture with a final 'm,' which has the form of a square without any opening,

147

to show that he will be born from the closed womb of a virgin.

There is also what we would today call a typographical error in the Bible. In the old manuscripts, as well as in modern scientific editions of the Hebrew Bible, the name Manaseh is written erroneously in Judges 18:30. Since there are no vowels in the original Hebrew, the word is written: M^NSH, with the N always appearing above the line of the text.

The explanation is that Jonathan, about whom this verse reports, was the first idolatrous priest in Israel. He was a grandson of Moses, written in Hebrew, MSH. The author of the book of Judges did not wish to shame the great legislator. He thought that respect for Moses' name was more important than accuracy in the genealogy of an idolater. So he added an N to the name of Moses, thereby changing it to Manaseh. For the few who have to know the whole truth and also to teach us how to communicate a truth in a diplomatic manner, the N is written above the line.

In the Bible inerrant? Yes, it is, even in its obvious errors. The truth is revealed from them too.

75: Qualified almightiness

If God is almighty, why does He not free us?

The Bible calls God 'Almighty' (Genesis 17:1, etc.). The Greek work for it is *pantocrator*, which means 'having power over all things.' Jerome translated the word into Latin with 'omnipotens,' which can be interpreted as meaning 'able to do anything.' The two concepts are not identical.

There are things which God cannot do. The Bible says, 'It was impossible for God to lie' (Hebrews 6:18). He cannot cease to exist. He himself has limited His sovereignty, and has given a Scripture which 'cannot be broken' (John 10:35). He cannot act contrary to his own character, or change his mind in essential things and say, 'I will not have love anymore,' or, 'there will be no righteousness and wrath in me.' There is therefore a 'must' even in God and in his providence.

As with God, so with man — we also 'must' pass through tribulations. Jesus says, 'The Son of man *must* suffer many things' (Luke 9:22), and again, 'Ye shall hear of wars and rumors of war. . . These things *must* come to pass' (Matthew 24:6).

Prayer is important, but its scope is limited. Speaking about the coming destruction of Jerusalem and Judaea, Jesus teaches his disciples, 'Pray ye that your flight be not in the winter, neither on the sabbath day' (Matthew 24:20), when it would be more difficult to find means of transportation. He does not say, 'Pray that the calamity itself should not come.' One could as well pray that 2 + 2 should not equal 4.

There exists a 'must.' When sins arrive at their peak, they bring with them unavoidable catastrophy, because it is in the unchangeable nature of God to punish sins. You can only ask for an alleviation of it.

God must have a certain character. What has no characteristics cannot exist.

How could we arrive at union with God if we could not be certain that He is on the peak toward which we advance? If there were no 'must' with God, we would strive to be holy and he might have changed to unholiness. He might even have changed his desire to be united with us.

God has power over all things. He is as the Bible calls him, pantocrator, but He has no power over His loving heart to make it cease beating for us. Our eye must be single (Luke 11:34), which means it must be the single eye. His eye and my eye are one.

The eye wherewith he sees me and my own eye are the same. The heavenly bridegroom says to his bride, 'Thou has ravished my heart with one of thy eyes' (Song 4:9), with the eye which is one and the same as his own.

God wished, wishes and will wish unity with us.

'Jesus Christ, the same yesterday, and today and for ever' (Hebrews 13:8).

76: Should a Christian defend his country?

Generally, it is dangerous to try to establish general rules by which a Christian should be guided. God has said, 'You shall be turned into another man and then let it be . . . that you do what is at your hand' (I Samuel 10:6–7 after the Hebrew), or as St Augustine said, 'Love and do what you like.'

Jesus said to the first generation of disciples, 'When ye shall see Jerusalem encompassed with armies . . . flee' (Luke 21:20–21). Many of us would have said, 'Then enlist in the army.' But a treasure of divine knowledge had been entrusted to the disciples which must not be lost. It was more important for the little band to defend this knowledge than to defend a fatherland which advanced toward destruction by God's decree.

Jeremiah, when the Jewish state was threatened by the Babylonians, delivered speeches which would today be considered high treason. He counseled surrender to the enemy without any resistance. Since the Jews were the chosen people, their mere survival was more important than the nobility of a heroic fight.

The occasions when such choices are necessary are

rare. No Christian would defend a Nazi Germany or a Communist Russia.

Otherwise the commandment of God stands, 'Let every soul be subject to the higher powers' (Romans 13:1). If your government has decided that a war is in the interest of the nation, you obey. It is not wrong to kill in a just war. 'After the return of Abraham from the slaughter of Chedorlaomer . . . Melchizedek, king of Salom (a type of Jesus) blessed him' (Genesis 14:17–19). Just this time had been chosen by Melchizedek to bless Abraham! Those who have fought against tyrannies are also blessed. The Christian can do much. Abraham with a small group of what we would today call 'freedom fighters' conquered world powers.

It is essential for children of God to participate in the fight against evil, even when this fight takes the form of war. Their role is 'to sanctify the war.' This is the expression used in the Hebrew of Joel 3:19. They should bring into the war the notions of righteousness and love. But foremost, the Christians' role is to prevent war, bringing the rulers of nations to living faith in Christ and teaching those who believe that the best guarantee of peace is strength.

77: The Name of God

Jesus says to God, 'I have manifested Thy name.' But which name did He manifest? Was it Jehovah, Elohim, El-Shadai, Lord of Hosts? There can be different explanations. May I suggest one.

When my wife was in Communist prisons, she brought one of her guards, let us call her Nina, to Christ. Sabina taught her the creed and the Our Father. One day this new Christian said to my wife, 'I cannot just repeat the Lord's prayer like a parrot. I must understand it. I say, "Hallowed be thy name," not knowing what His name is. Could you please tell me!' My wife answered, 'God has all names. In the Bible He is called God of Abraham, Isaac and Jacob. He is also God of Nina. He is your personal God. Nina is his name. Now sanctify it.'

The Biblical revelation goes even further. In both Hebrew and Greek the Bible text speaks not about a God *of* Abraham, *of* Isac and so on, but simply God Abraham, God Isac, God Jacob. He identifies himself with His friends and believers. It is not enough to believe that God is one. The Jews sing in the synagogue, 'Huh echad veein sheni.' (He is one and there is no second.) These words occur also in the Vedas. Each believer who comes to the One does not stop at being a second who obeys and adores the first, but becomes one with the One. God is God Abraham, and Abraham is Abraham God. Jesus says it, 'Ye are gods' (John 10:34).

The notion of oneness in Hebrew differs from that in the European languages. Man and wife shall be 'one flesh' (Genesis 2:24). In the Hebrew it is written about Samuel that 'he shall be Saul to the Lord' (I Samuel 1:28), which means he will feel so united with Saul that he will mourn when Saul fails. If Saul errs, Samuel will become twice as good to compensate for Saul's mistakes.

When Samuel died and went to the place of the righteous, he could assure Saul who had to die the next day, 'Tomorrow shalt thou and thy sons be with me' (I Samuel 28:19). Where else could Saul have gone after death? He had to be with Samuel because he was one with him. Samuel *was* Saul before God.

The unity between husband and wife is not a perfect one. Samuel and Saul clashed with each other, but deep underneath there was a unity which could not be sundered. Such is our unity with God. He is God Abraham, God Isac, God Nina, God Richard and God you. These are his names.

78: Scarcity of biographical data

No scrupulous modern biographer would attempt to write a biography of Jesus on the basis of the scarce data which the Bible gives about Him. Even about Jesus' earthly life we know next to nothing. Thirty years are passed over with silence. This is to show us that God keeps files on no one.

Job says, 'What is man . . . that thou shouldest try him every moment' (7:17)? What a man is in the present moment is what counts. What he has been before can be erased by the grace of God. Never hold past sins against a man, rather hold a man against his past sins.

George Muller, the British philanthropist, founder of many orphanages and renowned as a man of prayer, was in prison for theft in his youth. So was Skrefsrud, the renowned Norwegian missionary to the Santals in India.

St Vincent of Paul was ordained at the age of 19 although the Council of Trent had fixed 30 as the minimum age. He was silent all his mature life about his invalid ordination and about an adventurous escape from slavery which had occurred only in his imagination. He was also silent about the fact that in his youth he had sought the parishes with the fattest incomes.

What does an ugly past count, when God sees a beautiful present?

79: The Bible teaches poverty

When God makes Abraham a declaration of love, Abraham's answer is, essentially, 'what will you give me' Genesis 15:1–22)? Let it not be so with us. May we not be only parasites on God. May our relationship with Him not be all asking but also giving.

When you are converted you must become poorer than you were before, for Jesus' sake. Then when you purchase a dress, you can offer Him the difference in price between a plain and a fashionable one. Jesus has given his blood for me. Should I not offer Him everything I have?

Jesus forbids his disciples to have two coats (Matthew 10:10). What would He say about those who possess several houses and several cars?

The prophet Hosea had to buy his wife's love with money. Jesus is in the same predicament — He has had to buy his bride. Paul writes, 'Ye are bought with a price' (I Corinthians 7:23). The price paid for us is 'the precious blood of Christ' (I Peter 1:19). Would we sell ourselves to him for less? Would we give our lives to Him simply because He is right, even if He had no forgiveness of sins, no paradise and no earthly blessings to bestow? Are we his profiteers, or do we find in Him a beloved to whom to give our all?

Jesus said, 'Blessed be ye poor' (Luke 6:20). The strongest Greek word for poverty, *ptohois*, a word indicating abject misery, is used here.

The Lord asks the apostles, 'Do you not remember the five loaves *of the five thousand*' (Matthew 16:9)? The superfluous bread does not belong to me but to the poor.

George Muller who became a legend for the orphanages which he founded and supported by power of faith and prayer, wrote in his diary, 'We found the cheapest and plainest rooms in Bristol, but still too good for servants of Jesus. Our Master had nowhere to lay his head.'

As Jesus knelt to wash the feet of his disciples, St Hedwig of Silezia, a princess, gave gifts to the poor, kneeling before them. After such a life, Hedwig was able to say as her last word at her death, 'Welcome.'

Wealth is especially dangerous for ministers.

A journal of architecture published a photograph of the villa of a renowned American evangelist as being the most beautiful villa of the year. This man might have a better chance of preparing good sermons in a modest apartment.

I have heard sermons in cathedrals in rich countries and sermons delivered in prison by pastors in chains. The latter had the more durable influence upon my soul.

Rabbi Yehiel Meir, having no money to give a beggar, gave him one of his wife's rings. When the wife learned of it, she was upset, 'That was a very costly ring with a real diamond in it,' she said. Rabbi Yehiel, hearing this, searched the town for the beggar. He came home triumphantly and assured his wife, 'I found him and warned him to be sure to sell the ring for a good sum of money.'

Let us be souls who freely give ourselves with all we have to Him. Love poverty! Become poor.

80: Dove-like Israel

Israel and the Holy Spirit are both likened to a dove, as if to say that they belong to the same species. The Holy Spirit is God. We too are partakers of the divine dove-like nature (II Peter 1:4).

The Bridegroom says to the bride who is a symbol of his nation, 'you have doves' eyes' (Song 1:15). Why is Israel called a dove? 'Song of Songs Rabbah,' a Jewish book of wisdom explains: 'The dove is faithful. Israel was likewise faithful to the Holy One, praised be He, at Sinai. For they did not say that ten commandments, or twenty or thirty were enough for them, but they said, "All that the Lord has spoken we will do and be obedient" (Exodus 24:7). The dove is distinguishable among all other birds. Israel is likewise distinguished by deeds. The dove is modest. Israel is likewise modest. . . The dove does not leave its nest even if someone has taken its brood. Israel likewise continues to visit the temple site even though the Temple has been destroyed. The dove journeys and returns to its nest. Israel likewise "shall come eagerly like birds from Egypt and like doves from Assyria" (Hosea 11:11). Others are attracted to the dove; likewise, converts are attracted to Israel. The dove, unlike other birds, offers its neck for slaughter without struggling; children of Israel likewise give their lives for the Holy One, praised be He. The dove does not leave its mate, Israel likewise does not leave the Holy One, praised be He. The dove atones for sins. Israel likewise atones for the nations of the world.'

Belong to the dove, like Israel of God!

81: Humility

One of the main characteristics of a great man is his humility. Abraham is considered the father of all the faithful in the Jewish, Christian and Moslem religions. What was his opinion of himself? 'Behold, I am dust and ashes' (Genesis 18:27). David was a king, a poet, a man after God's heart. His opinion of himself? 'I am a worm, not a man' (Psalm 22:7).

We arrive nowhere without a humble acknowledgement of our unworthiness. A politician once asked a bishop, 'What can I do to obtain wisdom for ruling this country?' It was raining. The Bishop told him, 'Go outside in the rain for half an hour and stand with your head up in an unprotected place. The politican did this. When he returned, the bishop said, 'Did God grant you some wise instruction?' The man answered angrily, 'The only thing I could think about was that I am a fool.' The bishop nodded, 'Quite a discovery for a first try.'

Start like Paul with the recognition, 'I am an abortive' (I Corinthians 15:8, in the original). Only then will you be able to take upon yourself the burden of being famous. Sir Thomas Moore, martyred under Henry VIII of England, said, 'We must stand fast at the risk of being heróes.' Heroism is not something to be sought, but to be accepted though it endangers the more precious virtue of humility.

Remain humble, knowing that whatever your aims and however many skills you employ, you will not attain your earthly aims.

Engels was right when he wrote to the Russian revolutionist Vera Zasulitch on April 23, 1885, 'Men who bragged about having made a revolution, always realized next day that they did not know what they were doing, that the revolution performed had no resemblance to the one they intended. This is what Hegel called the irony of history, an irony only few historic personalities avoided.'

This applies not only to social revolutions. Not only have men like Lenin and Hitler died disappointed. Certainly the church is not what the church fathers intended. How unlike it is to the first church full of love in Jerusalem.

Luther intended a reformation within the Catholic church and died very unhappy about the chaos which

157

resulted from his efforts. Wesley too was disappointed. Mission founders have similar experiences.

Do not be proud. We are not made for successes, at least not for lasting ones. We are all shaped as vessels for the use of the Master. His purposes are fulfilled in our lives. 'It is God which works in you both to will and to do of his good pleasure' (Philippians 2:13).

Be humble and remember that even your humility does not come through your own merit. Then you will be a chosen vessel.

82: Strange commandment

You may sometimes wonder about the commandments God gives his prophets, whom men are taught to regard as models of life for their people. The first word which the Lord ever said to the prophet Hosea was, 'Take unto thee a wife of whoredoms and children of whoredoms' (1:2). Hosea complied. But why should a prophet have to do such a thing?

I believe the best explanation is given in the Talmud (Pesahim 87 a–b):

'The Holy One, praised be He, said to Hosea, "Your children have sinned." Hosea should have said, "They are your children, children of your dear ones, children of Abraham, Isaac and Jacob, show them your mercy." However, not only did he not say this, but he said, "Lord of the universe, the entire world belongs to You. Replace them with another people." The Holy One, praised be He, thought: "What shall I do with this old man? I shall tell him to marry a harlot and to beget children of harlotry and then I shall tell him to send her away. If he is able to send her away, I will send Israel away. And it is written, "The Lord said to Hosea, 'Go, take to yourself a wife of harlotry and have children of harlotry. . .' So he went and took Gomer." When two sons and a daughter had been born to him, the Holy One, praised be He, said to Hosea, "You must separate yourself from your wife." Hosea answered, 'Lord of the universe, I have children from her. I cannot put her away or divorce her." The Holy One said to him, "Your wife is a harlot and your children are children of harlotry. You do not even know if they are really yours. Yet you refuse to divorce her. How then, should I act toward Israel? They are the children of those whom I have tested, the children of Abraham, Isaac and Jacob, and one of the four possessions which I have acquired in My world: the Law, heaven and earth, the Temple and Israel. And yet you tell me to supersede them with another people."

'When he realized that he had sinned Hosea rose to ask mercy for himself. The Holy One, praised be He, said to him, "Before you ask mercy for yourself, ask mercy for Israel." '

None of the great men and women of God could be completely exempt from sin; they needed it. It was in the Providence of God that they should know it, so that their hearts would be soft for the multitude which sins. Taught by their own experience of life, they ceased to condemn, but began to intercede for those who trespass against the will of God.

You also may have received some strange guidance from God. Perhaps its purpose was to teach you humility.

83: Jesus incognito

Jesus often wished to keep incognito. He passed through Galilee with his disciples 'and he would not that any man should know it' (Mark 9:30). Might some people have Jesus near them even now, without knowing that it is He?

Angels too like to walk among men unrecognized. It is written: 'Be not forgetful to entertain strangers, for thereby some have entertained angels unaware' (Hebrews 13:2). Jesus is the Lord of angels — He might have taught them to pass incognito.

Like all who wish to remain hidden, Jesus uses pseudonyms. Even 'Jesus' is a pseudonym. Isaiah foretold that a virgin would bring forth a son 'and they shall call his name Emmanuel' (Isaiah 7:14). How can someone who does not bear this name be the person who fulfills the prophecy? If Mr Smith is announced, the arrival of Mr Taylor is not what you were entitled to expect. But before the birth of this child from a virgin, an angel tells Joseph, 'she shall bring forth a son and thou shalt call his name Jesus. . . . Now all this was done that it might be fulfilled which was spoken of the Lord by the prophet saying . . . they shall call his name Emmanuel' (Matthew 1:21–23). Strange.

Nor is the name 'Jesus' the last name which he will bear. Jesus appears to his apostle John saying that he who overcomes in the fight of faith will be made a pillar in the temple of God, and adding, 'I will write upon him my new name' (Revelation 3:12).

In eternity Jesus will have another name. *Jesus* (*Yeshuah*) in Hebrew, means 'Salvation.' In eternity there will be nobody to be saved. Apart from the name inscribed on those who overcome, He has a name written, that no man knew, but He himself' (Revelation 19:12). We say

'Jesus,' but this is only the name under which he made himself known to us. It is not his only name.

Even during his earthly life, Jesus did not always bear this name. 'When eight days were accomplished for the circumcising of the child, his name was called Jesus' (Luke 1:21). Until that time He had no earthly name. He was simply the Son of God incarnate, the Divine child. He could have been called by any name.

Scripture states, 'You shall keep my statutes and my judgments which if a man does, he shall live by them' (Leviticus 18:5). It is not written, 'which an Israelite' or 'which a believer in Christ' does, but 'a man,' any man. Scripture also says, 'This is the law of man' (II Samuel 7:19 in Hebrew). This is not the law of those who believe in the right name, but in the law of man, correct for all men. Although no man can be saved without knowledge of Jesus, there might be people who know Him and love Him as He walks among them incognito, under another name. There are people in all religions who in reality belong to Him.

84: Problems connected with death

I write the things below not as teaching, but to acquaint Western believers with the doubts and tempests in the spirit through which many Christians pass when in solitary confinement, with death reigning around them.

In Biblical perspective, death is not something to worry about. Perhaps chrysalises practice some funeral rite when one ceases to be among them, not knowing it had become a butterfly. So the believer passes at death to a higher stage.

We, the living, also remain in communion with them.

Luther abolished public prayers for the dead because such prayers had been abused for commerical purposes. Greedy priests sold indulgences which were supposed to help the dead escape torments.

However prayer mentioning the dead has a thorough Biblical foundation. Nehemiah prayed, 'Now therefore, our God . . . let not all the trouble seem little before thee that has come upon us, on our kings . . . and on our prophets' (9:32). When Nehemiah spoke these words, Israel no longer had kings. They were all dead, living in another sphere, but participating in what happened to Nehemiah's contemporaries. The troubles of the living Jews were shared by their former kings who had passed beyond death.

The verse is not always interpreted like this, but it can be understood in this manner.

The living also share in something which seems to be of great concern to the dead. Boaz said, 'Ruth the Moabitess . . . have I purchased to be my wife, to raise up the name of the dead upon his inheritance, that the name of the dead be not cut off from among his brethren' (Ruth 4:10).

It is important that we perpetrate in honor the names of our earthly predecessors and those who brought us to faith.

When I was in prison, I had the strong impression that three men who had been greatly influential in my conversion and were then dead, Isaac Feinstein, Christian Wolfkes and Giuseppe Cavane, were near me, imploring that I keep their good names through remaining faithful in tribulation. Let it be our concern 'that the name of the dead be not cut off from among his brethren.' Because Boaz took this care, the name of the dead husband of Ruth is mentioned in our Bible.

As a rule, dead saints are gathered unto their people (Genesis 49:33). They belong to the same church as we and we work together with them for salvation under our common head, Jesus Christ. The saints who have passed away 'are before the throne of God and serve Him day and night in his temple' (Revelation 7:15). But perhaps there is also another alternative.

We belong to the Body of Christ who gave himself for sinners. Perhaps we too can give ourselves for sinners. Paul wrote, 'I could wish that myself were accursed from Christ for my brethren, my kinsmen according to the flesh' (Romans 9:3). Moses also asked to be blotted out from the book of life if God would not forgive the Jewish people (Exodus 32:32). In principle this might be possible.

In his 95 Theses which started the Reformation, Luther, who believed in purgatory, approves of the popular belief that Popes Severinus and Paschal were willing to endure the pains of that place for the benefit of the faithful.

This is the concept of the Boddhisatva which is also found in Indian religion. The Boddhisatva is a man who refuses entry into the eternal bliss to which he is entitled, preferring to suffer and pray for those who, enmeshed in sin, have difficulty reaching this aim.

The question of our relationship with those who are on the other shore preoccupied us much in prison. Around us many, just the best died. We could be killed any moment. This made us to think in a manner apart, which probably would not be shared by Christians who lead the ordinary life.

My granddaughter told me: 'I enjoy being prayed for by many. I would not like to miss this joy in heaven.' Prayers for the dead might not be of any use to them, but should we do only what is useful?

85: Strange idiom

In the text of our Bibles it is clearly apparent that God is the author of all our calamities.

'God sold the Jews into the hands of Sisera, captain of the host of Hazor and into the hand of the Philistines and into the hand of the king of Moab' (I Samuel 12:9). Why should God deliver his people into the hands of his enemies?

God says through the prophet Jeremiah, 'I will cause to cease from the cities of Judah and from the streets of Jerusalem the voice of mirth and the voice of gladness' (Jeremiah 7:34). We learned that God is represented by Jesus who changed water into wine to give men pleasure. Yet He boasts of making joy vanish.

To understand those parts of Scripture which blame the evil upon God, we have to remember a peculiarity of the Hebrew language.

The Old Testament Joseph, when in prison with the butler and baker of Pharaoh, predicted to the one that he would be restored to Pharaoh's favor and to the other that he would be hanged. In the Hebrew original it is written that he, Joseph, 'restored the chief butler unto his office but hanged the chief baker' (Genesis 41:13). In fact, however, Joseph continued to remain in prison and took no part in the advancement of the one man, nor in the execution of the other. However, it is in the nature of the Hebrew language to call one who predicts or warns the 'author' of the respective action.

Jesus spoke with his disciples in Aramaean, a Hebrew dialect. When he told them, 'Whose soever sins ye remit, they are remitted unto them and whose soever sins ye retain, they are retained' (John 20:23), the words did not have the same meaning for them as they would for us. The words did not bestow upon the disciples an actual power to absolve or not to absolve sins. This power rests with God alone.

The apostles were called to proclaim the Gospel. Those who accepted their message would receive the divine pardon, the others not. The disciples were thus, as in the case of Joseph, the 'authors' of the forgiveness or lack of forgiveness of sin.

But now another question arises. The Hebrew language was fashioned by God to be a vehicle of his revelation. Why then does this idiom exist which gives the impression that the blame for evil lies on God just like the authorship of good? There is a deep meaning in it.

We usually hate men who wrong us and retaliate against them. God wishes to exonerate the wrong-doer in our eyes. He wishes that we harbor no bad feelings toward him. So he has formed his chosen language so as to give the impression that the tyranny of a Sisera in olden times or that of a Stalin or Hitler in modern times are His decision. Then we can love even the tyrants and their tools. Our account is only with God, and Him we love.

86: Do not brood about yourself

'Examine yourselves whether ye be in faith' (II Corinthians 13:5) is not the same thing as brooding about the state of your soul. Man is simply what he is just as every other element in nature. If you simply *are* what God created you to be, a creature in his image, nobody will ever call you to any account. 'No reckoning was made' with those who worked at the repair of the temple in Jerusalem 'because they dealt faithfully' (II Kings 22:7).

Man began to judge his own state and to discover that he was naked only after he had listened to the serpent in the garden of Eden instead of obeying God.

A greater percentage of women get cancer of the breast among those who continually check for it than among those who do not. The same danger lies in the self-examination and dissection of one's soul.

A thorough self-examination is not even possible, because you cannot be a judge in your own cause. This is an elementary rule of justice.

According to Gödel's incompleteness theory, no system can explain its own consistency without recourse to concepts that the system itself cannot generate. The criterion upon which you judge yourself must come not from your own mind, but from outside. But it remains your own mind which decides which outside criterion to adopt. Thus any attempt to judge yourself is futile. Men of different opinions judge themselves according to various criterions.

Hitler was sure he did well to exterminate the Jews. Jesus' judges were sure that they did well to sentence him. A sinner sins even in trying to determine his own sin and to evaluate true repentance.

Examine yourself only whether you have faith, as the Scriptures enjoin: whether you believe there is a greater intelligence than your own who has thought about everything, who shapes and directs your life; then enter into a calm attitude of mind.

The Hebrew word *avon* means 'sin' as well as 'punishment.' The very fact that you are a sinner is punishment enough, causing you to miss the inexpressible joys of righteousness. Do not add useless autoflagellation to your punishment.

There is a secret in your sinfulness. Cain, after killing his brother, says *Gadol avoni minso*, which, literally translated, is, 'My sin is great by its being borne' (Genesis 7:13).

'Though your sins be as scarlet, they shall be as white as snow' (Isaiah 1:18). The sins become white through the greatness of the sin-bearer. Because sin is in itself such a terrible punishment, Jesus took it upon himself. It was his joy to do so. To be a sin-bearer is his most beautiful crown. By entrusting your sins to him you add a jewel to his crown.

Examine yourself only to see if you are in faith, if you believe your sins to be white as snow because they now belong to Jesus, and, with this, enter into peace.

87: The red dragon

'Behold a great red dragon' (Revelation 12:3). Why is this dragon, whose intent is to devour the Christ child, colored red?

Sin is also associated with red. It would seem that to speak about the color of sin would have as much sense as speaking about the melody of a fruit, but God says, 'Let us reason together. Though your sins be as crimson, they shall be as wool' (Isaiah 1:18). So sin is red and righteousness is white.

It was no accident that Communism and Nazism, the two great anti-Christian movements of our age, both chose red flags. Not only did they fulfill a prophecy, but the choice also derived from a source deep within the experience of mankind.

The French psychologist Alfred Binet related an experiment with a hysterical woman whose body was paralysed on one side. When a dynamometer was placed in her right hand she could squeeze it to register only 12 kg. If she was shown a red disk, the pressure of her squeeze was immediately doubled (in 'Researches about the alterations of conscience with hysterical persons' *Philosophical Magazine*, vol. 17/1889, France).

Goethe, who developed a theory of light, also attributed dynamic character to the color red, which he distinguished as being an active color.

Every color is a suffering of light, because colors are produced by light breaking through a prism. Red is its greatest suffering.

Animals can be driven mad by showing them a piece of red cloth. Toreadors make use of this fact in bullfighting. All primitive people have a predilection for red, and so do little children.

White is not actually a color, but the fullness of light, light which has not passed through a prism. The righteous will stand before Christ, the lamb of God, clothed in white (Revelation 12:9). In contrast to the violent color of revolutionists and persecutors, to the color of the dragon, white is the color of quietness, of contemplation, the good part chosen by Mary of Bethany (Luke 10:42).

The servants of the red dragon delight in the sight of blood. Persecutors have shed rivers of martyrs' blood. The righteous, on the other hand, are givers of life.

In a world dominated or terrorized by the red dragon, in a world where love is scarce and relationships are icy, the righteous bring the warmth of love.

No scientist can explain how it is that a stream of warm water, the Gulf stream, flows between the cold waters of the ocean, which, so to speak, form its walls, how that moving hot stream exists within the motionless cold. So the righteous, clothed in white, journey toward heaven through a world inhabited by passionate red monsters, a world which is by contrast with the radiant love of the righteous, icy and cold.

88: Strange expressions in the Hebrew Bible

Biblical Hebrew is a very poor language, with only 400 word stems. For this reason it contains many homonyms and strange expressions which we often find contain spiritual messages. A few examples follow.

Elisha asks his teacher Elijah, 'Let a double portion of thy spirit be upon me.' There is of course no quantitative measurement of spirit, so these words might seem senseless, but among the Jews, the eldest son commonly received a double portion of inheritance. Thus Elishah's words imply, 'Make me your principal spiritual heir.'

Some adversaries of the Jews wrote a letter to the Persian king Artaxerxes, saying among other things, 'We are salted with the salt of the palace' (Ezra 4:14 in the Aramean original). Salt of the palace is an expression for salary from the king. The English word 'salary' also derives from 'salt.'

We read, 'Saul was the son of one year in his reign' (I Samuel 13:1 in Hebrew). This was a manner of saying that he was childish as a ruler.

The Hebrew has no special word for 'period.' The word *iom* is used for both 'period' and 'day.' So, from the Biblical text it cannot be established whether God created the world in six days or in six periods.

Kavod means both 'glory' and 'heavy.' These homonyms express the spiritual truth that it is a glory to carry heavy burdens for the love of God.

Lekoneh means 'to get as result of a relationship of love' or 'to conceive.' Eve says, *Qanithi*, 'I got a man from the Lord,' when she gave birth to her first son (Genesis 4:1). Later on the word became used for 'buying.' The Jews did not intend commerce to be a cold, selfish transaction, but rather a relationship in which, governed by love, two parties exchange needed items. Let Christian merchants profit by this teaching.

Leshaal means 'to ask' as well as 'to lend.' Thus, to lend (leshaal) to everyone who asks (shaal) is a teaching inherent in the very fiber of the Hebrew language.

The name of the first king of Israel, Saul (Sheoul in Hebrew) means 'lent.' Therefore 'as long as he (Samuel) lives, he shall be lent to the Lord' (I Samuel 2:28), could also be correctly translated, 'Samuel shall be Saul to the Lord.' One man can take another's place before God.

Hattath means both 'sin' and 'sin-offering.' God said to Cain, 'If thou doest not well, *hattath* lies at the door.' It is well for every man who has committed *hattath*, a sin, to remember that by so doing he has brought Jesus, the sin-offering, near to him, ready to forgive. Thus Jesus, too, is me before God as Samuel was Saul.

The Bible speaks about men baptized for the dead (I Corinthians 15:29). When certain Christians were martyred, others who had wavered until that time, encouraged the martyrs' example of faith, came to take their place in the church and became baptized.

When a believer fails, another can, through fasting, mourning, praying, and working twice as hard as before, make good the loss which the Kingdom has endured. Therese of Avila taught 'When you see a sister sinning, be thou much holier so that God may receive the same amount of love.' Samuel practised this substitution for Saul, and in this sense, Samuel was Saul before God.

You too can be a shield for another before God, replacing through your excellence in faith someone else's frailty.

89: Punishment for children

Little children mocked Elisha and said unto him, 'Go up, thou bald head, go up, thou bald head. And he turned back and looked on them and cursed them in the name of the Lord. And there came out two she bears out of the wood and tare forty two children of them' (II Kings 2:24).

What the children were mocking was probably not just baldness, but perhaps something like the tonsure of Catholic priests in times before or the tonsure of the Oriental religions, which may have been used by Jewish prophets. But why such harsh a punishment for a childish prank?

Our modern concept is that a child cannot be held responsible for wrong behaviour. Everything is blamed on society, family, school, or the police; children's crimes are usually attributed to poverty, although the majority of poor children do not commit crimes, and many offenders have more money than those they rob.

The ancient Jews believed however that a child should not commit crimes, a child should not steal, should not mock religion and if he does, he should receive due punishment.

Still, why was the punishment so severe?

Jews believe that Elijah still walks on earth in disguise, and one legend tells of a man who asked to walk beside him to learn from him the ways of God. In beggars' rags, they sought hospitality at a poor man's house. The poor man received them in a friendly way and shared the milk of his only cow with them. In the morning, leaving the house, Elijah cursed the cow and it died. The second night they asked hospitality of a rich man. The rich man spoke harshly to them and sent them, without food, to sleep in his barn. In the morning Elijah advised the man to dig in a certain place and the rich man found treasure buried there. Later Elijah and his companion met a child, who kindly went out of his way to give directions. When they passed a bridge, Elijah pushed the boy into the river where he drowned. At last Elijah's companion could not bear it any longer and asked for explanations. Elijah said, 'the cow I cursed had anthrax. If I had not killed it, the family would have been poisoned. The rich man whom I made even richer, although he was bad, was involved in big financial speculations. The treasure will encourage him to even wilder schemes with the result that in the end he will lose everything he has. The loss will make him wiser and soften his heart. In the good child I saw criminal tendencies. He would have destroyed his soul and broken the hearts of his parents, had he continued to live. I saved him by giving him death.'

There are men like Elijah with special endowments from God who can see criminality in children before it has developed, as botanists distinguish what future flower will grow from what to us is just a seed. Only such enlightened men are licensed to a severity forbidden the ignorant. Elijah was as entitled to do what he did as a doctor who could diagnose a fetus as abnormal would be justified in performing an abortion.

It is not correct for those who are ignorant to judge prophets. We should rather learn from them to maintain a careful watch over our children and never to prefer our children to God. If they sin, they must be punished, and, in extreme cases, rejected.

Children are responsible for what they do. As St Therese of Avila sought martyrdom among the moors at the age of seven, so a wicked child must atone for his wickedness.

90: Learn from flowers

Christians should know something about flowers. Jesus taught 'Consider the lilies' (Matthew 6:28). He calls himself 'the rose of Sharon and the lily of the valleys' (Song of Solomon 2:1). Without this Biblical teaching, we would never have had Masefield's lyric at the end of 'The Everlasting Mercy.'

'O lovely lily clean,
O lily springing clean,
O lily bursting white,
Dear lily of delight
Spring in my heart again
That I may flower to men.'

We can learn from flowers not to be disturbed that the Christians are constituted of so many denominations. There are 35,000 species of orchids alone.

The number of Christian denominations has to increase even more. Our ultimate hope is for every believer to be an Abraham, a friend of God and a man under God's direct guidance, each to be his own denomination. Men differ from each other. Each person will have his own gifts and visions, and uniting them will be a profound love which transcends their differences of view.

Flowers do not quarrel with each other. The right relationship between denominations and believers is mutual admiration.

Secondly, every flower is wisdom personified. Orchids are masters in adopting different shapes for the purpose of multiplication.

The Mediterannean's Ophrys resembles a female wasp and emits a similar odor to attract the male wasp. In the wasp's attempt to mate with the plant, he picks up pollen masses, which eventually brush off onto another flower. The Santa orchid has a platform which resembles a nectar-bearing flower, so it attracts bees in search of nectar which it does not have.

Australia's flying-duck orchid springs a trap when an insect lands on its lips. With a jerk, the orchid tosses the intruder into a cup formed by petals around a green column. The escaping insect carries away pollen masses to deposit on the next flower.

Other orchids display other curiosities to attract specific pollinators (*National Geographic Magazine*).

Christians also wish to multiply. Paul writes, 'Unto the Jews I became as a Jew, that I might gain the Jew; to them that are under the law, as under the law, that I might gain them that are under the law; to them that are without law, as without law . . . to the weak became I as weak, that I might gain the weak. I am made all things to all men, that I might by all means save some' (I Corinthians 9:20–22).

Christianity has an amazing multitude of approaches, all of them correct so long as we pursue the one aim: ever to increase the church of Christ.

91: Lesser known personalities of the Bible

Paul writes to the Romans, 'Erastus, the chamberlain of the city salutes you' (Romans 16:23). An inscription was found in excavations at Corinth, 'Erastus, procurator, aedile, laid the pavement at his own expense.' According to archaeological evidence the pavement is from the middle of the first century. The identity of name, location and date make it likely that the subject is the same person ('A Guide to the excavations of ancient Corinth,' American School of Classical Studies, Athens, 1936). To receive a greeting from such a person, one who does not profit of his position to enrich himself, but, on the contrary, spends from his pocket for a public need, would be an honor indeed.

Gamaliel is the only New Testament name also celebrated by the Talmud, a book commonly opposed to Christianity. It is believed that Gamaliel's father, Simeon, was the old man who took the baby Jesus in his arms and said the prayer, 'Nunc dimittis' (Luke 2:25–35). His grandfather was the renowned rabbi Hillel. Gamaliel was so honored that he is one of seven Jewish teachers to whom the name 'Raban' was given, a title also born by Jesus. Magdalene addressed him as 'Rabbuni.'

Gamaliel was also called 'the beauty of the Law.'

Unlike other Pharisees, he was not a bigot. It is said that he once bathed in Greece in a place where a statue of a heathen goddess stood. Reproached for this, he silenced his critics by saying that the bath was not built for the goddess, who does not have the habit of washing herself, but for men, the statue serving as ornament.

Gamaliel was Paul's teacher of religion. He also undertook the defense of St Peter when persecuted.

His attitude toward Christianity fluctuated. After a period of mild tolerance he became its passionate adversary. He composed a prayer against the Hebrew Christians which is still recited three times daily in Orthodox synagogues: 'Let there be no hope to them that apostate from true religion, and let heretics, how many so ever may be, all perish as in a moment. And let the kingdom of pride be speedily rooted out and broken in our days. Blessed art thou, O Lord our God, who destroyest the wicked and bringest down the proud' (Home, 'Introduction to Scriptures' 8th ed., vol. III, p. 261, quoted in 'The Life and Epistles of St Paul' by W Conybeare, Scranton & Co., Hartford, 1900).

Archaeologist, however, discovered that Gamaliel's tomb bears a Christian inscription, indicating that toward the end of his life he received Christ as his Savior.

175

92: Sources of the Bible

The Bible is not entirely a direct revelation from God. It contains quotations from numerous other books, some of which are known.

Jude quotes two apocryphal books in his epistle. The story told in verse 9 that Archangel Michael contended with the devil about the body of Moses comes from the book, 'Assumption of Moses.' The saying in verse 14, 'The Lord comes with ten thousands of his saints to execute judgment upon all,' is a quote from the book of Enoch.

In Acts 17:28, St Paul quotes the Greek poet Eratus. Since Eratus, like Paul, was a native of Cilicia, it was natural that Paul be familiar with his writings. Eratus was renowned for his astronomical poems, and Ovid declared that his reputation would endure as long as the sun and moon. Eratus' only lasting reputation however is that Paul quoted from one of his poems: 'Thou who amid the immortals are throned the highest in glory, Giver and Lord of life, who by law disposes of all things; Known by many a name, yet the almighty forever; Hail, O Zeus, for to thee should each mortal voice be uplifted. Offspring are we too of thine, we and all that is mortal around us.'

How many preachers today would dare quote the Book of Mormon or the Koran as freely as Paul quotes this ode to the heathen deity Zeus, a poem which proclaims that not only men but all that is mortal, including animals and plants, are God's offspring?

Paul also quotes three other Greek poets. From Aratus he takes the words, 'In God we live, we move and have our being' (Acts 17:28). The saying, 'Evil communications corrupt good manners' (I Corinthians 15:33), is a line from 'Thais,' a comedy of Menander, and could well have become a proverb.

'The Cretians are always liars, evil beasts, slow bellies' (Titus 1:12), is from Epimenides of Crete (8th century B.C.), whose sayings were considered prophetic. Plato called Epimenides a divinely inspired man and Plutarch called him a man dear to God, but his harsh judgment against a whole nation certainly does him no honor.

Judgmental generalizations about a people should be avoided, but they lose their sharpness if they come from a son of that nation. The Jewish prophets spoke harshly about the Jews, and Luther about the Germans. Their intentions were beneficent.

Even great artists can sometimes write on a low intellectual level. It is correct to show respect towards poets and men of letters not only when they are at their peak, but even when they fail, as Paul shows Epimenides in this instance.

These are but a few examples of the sources from which the authors of Scripture took some of their inspiration.

93: The Phoenicians

Most Christians are aware of their debt to the Jews in matters of knowledge of God. We also owe much to another Biblical nation, the Phoenicians. They were among the Canaanites, and are also called in the Bible by the names of their cities, Sidonians, or Tyrians. The Greeks gave them the name, Phoenicians. Jesus speaks of them favorably as compared with the sinfulness predominant in Jewish cities of the time (Matthew 11:21).

The Phoenicians were the first people to introduce an alphabet as we now know it, with 22 symbols for different sounds (as in the Hebrew, they had no letters for vowels). This was a great advance over the hieroglyphs of the Egyptians or the cuneiform characters of Mesopotamia. When you read your Bible, remember that we learned our alphabet from the Phoenicians.

The word for our holy book, 'Bible' is a phoenician word. These people had a town named Byblos which was renowned for its trade in papyrus and for its use of script. Eventually the idea 'book' became identified with the name of the town. When rabbies translated the Hebrew writings into Greek for the first time, they gave the book the name 'Bible.'

The Hebrews had exact indications from God about building a sanctuary to Him, but they did not know how to construct such huge edifices. They learned it from the Phoenicians, from Hiram, King of Tyre (I Kings 5).

The Lebanese of today are the successors of the Phoenicians. Remembering in love the heritage we received from the Jews, let us remember in love this people also.

94: The need for theological clashes

Paul quarreled with Peter and Barnabas in matters involving doctrine and church leadership. He taught us to reject heretics (Titus 3:10). Apostle John likewise advises us not to receive into our house anyone who brings a false doctrine. (II John 10).

In later ages the difference between Christian truth and heresy became blurred. At Interlaken, Switzerland, two rivers merge, one thick with salt and mud, and other

pure. For a time they run in the new bed without min-
gling, as if there were a border between them. But finally
they merge. The mud triumphs, invading everything.

It is difficult to distinguish water from mud, but this
filtration must be made. Truth alone sets free. Theological error only compounds bondage. Debates and clashes
on religious issues were not avoided in the time of the
apostles and they cannot be avoided now.

Immediately after the Reformation the newly found
Protestant church was torn by four main theological
quarrels:

(1) The fight against antinomians led by Agricola.
Nomos is the Greek word for law. The antinomians
asserted that law should only be the business of
magistrates, and should play no role in religion.
Luther opposed them, saying that law comes from
God and must be respected under the new
covenant.

(2) Schwenkfeld and Osiander did not believe that
Christ's righteousness can be ascribed to us. They
believed that in order to be justified before God,
we must have an essential righteousness of our
own, and that Christ cannot manifest himself fully
in us because of our inherent sinfulness. Luther
taught to rely totally on Christ for our salvation.

(3) A professor Major and Amsdorf went so far in
denying any human merit in salvation that they
declared good deeds as harmful for those who wish
to obtain eternal life. Luther believed that good
deeds are the natural fruits of faith.

(4) The great synergetic quarrel started by Melan-
chthon who granted the human will a part in our
salvation. Our will for the good, he said, is not
dead, but only sick, and can still co-operate with
the Holy Spirit. In opposition to him Flavius believed that fallen man can only oppose divine en-
deavour, and God forces us to be saved. Luther
kept the golden middle with his doctrine that our

will plays no active role in salvation, but can participate by suffering, receiving, and accepting it.

We have to endure theology and pass beyond it to love our brethren. Theology can only be endured. It is repugnant to make the word of God matter of debate, most often of low quality. But there are many repugnant things a man cannot avoid. We have to orientate ourselves among the different tendencies in religious thought. If we are unable to recognize heresy, neither will we be able to discern the truth.

We therefore have to accept the strife among believers both in the past and those today, but in this, as in all other matters, right measure is the most important Christian virtue.

95: The holiness of sex

In the modern world the sexual organs are commonly the objects of greedy desire, obscenity and dirty jokes. In Biblical times the sexual organ was held in such honor that oaths were given on it, as today some people would swear on the Bible or on the crucifix. 'Abraham said unto his eldest servant . . . Put, I pray thee, thy hand under my thigh and I will make thee swear' (Genesis 24:203).

The usual Biblical name for the male organ is 'vessel,' and for the female, *boshet*, or 'shame,' in the sense that it is shameful to speak about it in a degrading manner.

These are the organs of procreation. Understand clearly the meaning of this word. We *pro-create*. We create in behalf of God. When God wishes another human being, he assigns a male and female the high calling of creating it. Among the people of God, sexual union is considered sacred. Isaiah wrote, 'I took unto me faithful witnesses to record, Uriah the priest and Zechariah the son of Jeberechiah, and I went unto the prophetess and she conceived' (8:1–2). In this instance the sexual act was performed like a religious ceremony, under the supervision of a priest.

The standard of social justice in the Bible was high, with the result that there was no occasion for sexual impurity in Israel. Today rich men contribute to sexual immorality not only by overt sexual wrongs, but by driving thousands of girls into prostitution by paying unjust wages.

The New Testament begins by recording a long series of sexual acts: 'Abraham begot Isaac and Isaac begot Jacob' and so on (Matthew 1:2). Some of these unions were illegitimate, but what distinguished them all from ordinary sexual intercourse was the aim pursued in them. Abraham begot *Isaac*.

Modern people mate without giving any thought to the personality which might result. But Abraham and Sarah's purpose was to bring into life a child of a certain character who would further bear the seed of the Messiah to come.

Leah, when she was past the age of bearing, gave her handmaid to her husband that the holy seed of Jacob should not be lost. Later she herself gave birth to a son, saying, 'God hath given he my hire, because I have given my maiden to my husband' (Genesis 30:9–18).

Let us also treat sexuality with deep respect; let us procreate with reverence and for the purpose of bringing new servants of God into the world.

This does not mean however that sexual union should not be pleasurable. Dietrich Bonhoeffer expressed it well when he wrote, 'To long for the transcendent when you are in your wife's arms is, to put it mildly, a lack of taste, and it is certainly not what God expects of us. We ought to find God and love him in the blessings he sends us. If he pleases to grant us some overwhelming earthly bliss, we ought not to try to be more religious than God himself.'

96: Unusual letters in the Bible

The original manuscripts of the Bible do not have upper and lower case letters; all letters are of equal size. However there are some exceptions in Hebrew which have nothing in common with English orthographic rules prescribing the use of capital letters for God, proper names or the names of countries. In the German language, *all* substantives begin with a capital letter.

In the Hebrew Old Testament, only some 35 places are letters of unusual size used, either bigger, smaller or above the line, to alert the reader to special paragraphs which were considered very important. For example, in Ruth 3:13, the word 'lini' which means tarry is written with a bigger 'L' because it is very necessary for believers to learn to tarry. Boaz said to Ruth at midnight, 'Tarry this night, and it shall be in the morning. . .' In other words, do not be in a hurry. Do not try to achieve things under adverse circumstances. *Tarry*. A beautiful morning will come; Boaz will marry Ruth; David and later on Jesus will be descendants of this marriage. 'Tarry' is written here with the only bigger 'L' in the Bible.

Jesus believed not in the verbal but the literal accuracy of Scripture. He said, '. . . one jot or one title shall in no wise pass from the law . . .' (Mt. 5:18). Historic events since then have proved that He was right.

St Athanasius fought against the heretic Arius for an

'i.' Arius said that Christ is 'homoiusios,' of similar substance with the Father. Athanasius said that He is 'homousios', of the same substance. Had Arius' 'i' been accepted, the whole Church would have gone astray.

Believe in every letter of Scripture, even the size. It is no accident that the Communists oblige people to write 'God' with a small 'g,' and that Solzhenitsyn refused to have his novel published if the word were not printed with a capital 'G.'

97: What is the truth?

The Hebrew word for truth, *Emeth*, is used for many other notions which, if practised, bring the truth with them. *Emet* also means 'perseverance,' 'reliability,' or 'faithfulness.' It is impossible to attain to the truth without possessing these qualities as well. Persevere in forgiveness and humility, enable God to rely on your self-denial, and you will not have to seek truth. It will seek you.

A girl had an illegitimate child. Wishing to shield her lover from the anger of her father, she accused the pastor of being the guilty one. The girl's father came to church one Sunday morning with the baby, thrust it into the arms of the pastor and shouted, 'Here, villain, take your bastard. You are a whoremonger.' Astonished, the congregation waited for the pastor to defend himself. Instead he caressed the child and said, 'So be it! What a beautiful boy. I will give him all my love.' From then on the congregation shunned him. Earning his living by manual labor, he cared for the child. After many years, the girl felt remorse and confessed the truth to her father. The following Sunday the father publicly apologized to the former pastor who now sat on a bench in the rear of the church. 'I apologize. I have been misguided; you are completely innocent' the father said. The pastor replied, 'So be it. A handsome boy. I really like him. He is mine.' Still not a word in his own defense; no explanation!

Faithfulness to the One who, when reviled, did not revile in return, who was silent before Pilate, though accused of the worst crimes. Men like this have the privilege of truth in religious matters.

But how much truth do these have?

What did Jesus mean when he said 'I am the truth'? (John 14.6).

We have the truth in matters which can be repeated experimentally or about facts which can be documented unchallengeably. We have certain truths in mathematics, physics, etc. In most matters, objective truth is still beyond our reach.

A person must be very daring to assert he has the final objective truth in religion. Northern Europe is Lutheran; the Southwest is Catholic; the East, Orthodox; India, Hindu and the Middle East, Moslem. Can truth be geographically conditioned?

The most murderous influence in religious history has been the assumption of objective truth in religion. We have to live with relative truth, accepted by our minds as result of long heritage, education, climate, circumstances of life, and the interplay of historical events. As in other domains, we must rely largely on probability in some religious matters, too.

Some have broken with their heritage and have converted from other religions to Christianity. But how many religions did one examine before becoming a Christian? Converts are also limited in their choices. Biblical religion was inherited, not a matter of personal choice. Such expressions as 'personal acceptance of Christ' or 'a personal Savior' do not occur in the Scriptures. One cannot even find the word 'personal.' This may seem strange for modern believers who scoff when a man is Catholic or Protestant because it is the religion of his parents, without a personal search for the truth.

Biblical religion was also collective. One belonged first to a nation into which one was born, the Jewish one. Later one belonged to a collectivity, the church, which was advised to 'bring up the children in the nurture and admonition of the Lord' (Ephesians 6:4), not leaving them to make the impossible choice among hundreds of religions when they became mature. Jude sets as our aim not a personal but a 'common salvation' (Jude 3). At maturity you consciously adhere to what has been infused into you since birth.

Abraham's son, Ishmael was circumcised at the age of thirteen by his own consent. Another son, Isaac, received circumcision at the age of eight days, according to God's commandment. He decided nothing. His parents chose to enter him into the covenant with the Creator.

Reason made Ishmael practise a rite. Reason later caused him to mock his brother, the bearer of God's promises. Isaac received his religion not by personal choice, but through God's grace as bestowed upon a family called to become a great nation. He was God's choice. He possessed the truth.

Jesus *is* the truth in the sense that He always embodied the truth He taught. Jesus was *identical* with the road He walked, completely satisfied with the life he led. Therefore he IS the life.

We, on the other hand, are always in conflict with the truth we recognize; we hate the ways we have chosen for ourselves, or to which existence has led us and we are dissatisfied with our lives. In contrast with this sinful attitude of ours, Jesus embodies complete acceptance of what God allotted to Him as human knowledge and way of life. He had no inner conflict about the problems of existence. Let us follow Him in this.

If we can be faithful and persevere in following the small truths we know, the greater truth will gladly come to abide in us.

98: The legitimacy of questioning

The Bible is full of questions put to God. Jeremiah asks, 'Wherefore doest thou forget us for ever and forsake us for so long time?' (Lamentation 5:20). The book concludes without answer, with the discouraging words, 'Thou has utterly rejected us, thou art very wroth against us' (v. 21).

Woe to a faith which does not question. Reason questions everything it sees and hears. Only a reason undedicated to God does not question who He is and what He does and what His intentions are. The answers we receive are as inconclusive as those of science. If matter and its constituent particles, the atoms, are mysterious, the more so is God, their creator. He has given us a revelation which would not be worthy of Him if it were not also enigmatic.

The whole of reality can be comprehended only with the whole of our being. When we try to understand it with so small a part of ourselves as the intellect, it is unavoidable that we fail.

What is our relationship to God? Has he predestined everything? If so, what is our responsibility?

Jesus tells the parable of the sower. 'A sower went out to sow his seed, and as he sowed, some fell by the wayside . . . some fell upon a rock . . . some among thorns . . . others on good ground' (Luke 8:5–8). The harvests were brought in accordingly. In succeeding verses of the same chapter it is clearly revealed that the seeds symbolize different types of men.

We have been made to live in different circumstances with different innate characteristics, more or less favorable to spiritual development. Before ever sinning ourselves, we have been sinned against through the genes transmitted to us, through erroneous upbringing, or through others' mistakes. Other people, through no seeming merit of their own, have been privileged in heredity, education and experiences of the world.

God said, 'Jacob have I loved and Esau have I hated . . . the children not being yet born, neither having done any good or evil, that the purpose of God according to election may stand' (Romans 9:11–13). This means that the essential character, the seed, and the conditions, the soil, are determined.

But if we are destined to fall by the wayside where the fowls of the air can devour the seed, since we have been created with intelligence, could we not erect a scarecrow and save ourselves? If arid soil has been our allotment, could we not irrigate and fertilize?

It is natural that human reason questions whether everything is predestination or if there exists a bit of space for free will. The apocryphal book of Jesus ben Sirah replies: 'Do not research things which surpass your mind, and do not try to know things which are hidden. Reflect about things which are permitted; do not be busy with what is mysterious.'

Mishna, a Jewish book of wisdom, says, 'For whomsoever tries to solve the following four problems, "What is above, what is below, what has been before the beginning of the world and what will be its end" — for those who do not respect the secrets of Godhead, it would have been better not to be born.'

It is normal to ask questions and normal to shrink back from the depths these questions open. We will never fathom them. Therefore, although we continue to ask, we seek no answers in this life to all the questions, but just trust in a God of love.

If we can also rejoice in the fact that we have no answers, this shows we have reached the great truth known, alas, by few: the whole universe and all of life are great question marks. There can be no replies in this world, but only in the next.

A child in elementary school sometimes asks amazingly profound questions, answers to which cannot begin to be understood until the child reaches the university.

Let us wait patiently for life eternal and in the meantime let us act vigorously in love. All the whys and ifs will not help. Ask instead, 'What can I do?' and 'How can I improve on what I am?'

One of the answers you will receive at once is: 'Rejoice about the existence of ever-to-be-asked and never-to-be-answered questions, about the whys and whethers. They are proof that we are not made only for earthly life but for eternity. For the time being, let it be with us as it is in the life of trees. To their questions, branches respond with flowers and fruits, not with words. Make roses blossom even on your crosses.'

99: Is the first chapter of the Bible wrong?

God said, 'Let there be light' on the first day of creation (Genesis 1:3). Critics disparage the Bible on this account, asserting there cannot be light without the sun, which appeared only on the fourth day. But God who could make the glowworm, phosphorescent matter and the aurora borealis, could surely cause light before making the sun.

Upon close examination, the words about the creation of light on the first day have a deeper sense, as does the whole first chapter of the Bible. I reproduce below the opening passage in Hebrew with the word for word translation in English:

Bereshit bara Elohim et hashamaim ve-et haarets

In the beginning created God (et) the heavens and (et) the earth.

This is the word for word translation except for *et*, a word which has no English equivalent. This was originally written in Hebrew with the mute sound *alef* and the *tav*, which is like our 't.' The vocalizations were added in the Hebrew Bible only after many centuries. Aleph-tav could also stand for *ot*, in which case the sentence would read, 'In the beginning God created; a sign of this creation would be the heavens, and another sign, the earth.' Such a translation would rightly convey the sense of the text, but would be open to question because, although *ot* can be written aleph-tav, it is usually written aleph-vav-tav.

If we do not accept this explanation of the word *et*, the problem of its meaning remains. The renowned Jewish medieval commentator Ibn Ezra says, 'The particle *et* signifies the substance of the thing.' Another Jewish scholar, Kimchi, agrees, adding that *aleph* and *tav* are the first and last letters of the alphabet. *Et* therefore indicates the beginning and end of all things (like the Alpha and Omega in Greek).

The meaning of the Bible's first sentence is then, 'In the beginning God created the substance of heaven and earth.' The Syriac version conveys this idea. St Ephrtem the Syrian's interpretation too is on these lines. God did not create a finished universe, but its essence, open to development. Such an interpretation would also elucidate the problem of the creation of light on the first day.

Nothing has a greater velocity than light. Thus God started the essence of the universe by creating the entity which has the greatest speed.

God said, 'Let there be light' ie. 'Let us hurry with great speed towards the perfect kingdom!'

Later God said, 'Let there be a firmament' (Genesis 1:6). The word firmament suggests some kind of fixed vault dividing the skies from earth. The Hebrew text here uses the word *rakiah*, best translated, 'expanse,' because it has as root a verb which means 'to stretch out.' This rendering of the word *rakiah* also ties in with the notion of a universe created in its essence. Far from suggesting a firm vault, the idea of *rakiah* is a splendid presentiment of the modern theory according to which the universe is continually expanding, stretching out.

If a source of light is becoming nearer to you, then the whole spectrum of the light is shifted towards the violet; if the source is becoming more distant, then the whole spectrum is shifted towards the red, like the pitch of a train whistle which changes according to whether the train is approaching or receding.

The nearest cluster of stars which is about 43 million light-years away, and which contains about 2,500 galaxies, has a shift corresponding to a speed of recession from us of 750 miles a second. The most distant cluster so far investigated has a red-shift over one hundred times as great, corresponding to a speed of recession which is almost half of the speed of light.

Thus does science report exactly what the Bible says, 'God created heavens and stretched them out' (Isaiah 42:5).

The first chapter of the Bible is right. God created the *rakiah*. Moreover, the fact that the story of creation starts with the making of light before the sun proves the Divine authorship of the Bible, for no human author would want to create such difficulties for himself.

100: About prayer

Jesus taught us to cry day and night toward God (Luke 18:7). However God should not be likened to some unrighteous judge from whom justice can be obtained only by wearing him out with insistent pleas.

Why is it written, 'Pray ye the Lord of the harvest that he will send forth laborers into his harvest'? (Matthew 9:38). If He is full of love, why does He not simply provide the laborers without waiting for our prayer?

We pray in order to obtain clarity. Only a life of prayer will teach you that neither questioning God nor theology have any part in prayer. Prayer will teach you to pass your life in silence, at the bosom of a God whom we cannot fully understand.

When extreme need or threat arises, it is good to cry. Nobody whispers when threatened by a dragon. God says to Samuel, 'their cry has come unto me' (I Samuel 9:16). If the cry is missing, the realization of our great danger in this valley is missing. But after the cry the silence returns.

It is a good Biblical custom to ask for signs from God. Jonathan says to his arms bearer, 'If the Philistines tell us, "Tarry until we come unto you, then we will stand still in our place . . ." but if they say thus, come up unto us, then we will go up, for the Lord has delivered them into our hand' (I Samuel 14:9–10). Ask for certain concrete things, as Jonathan asked for guidance in initiating a battle against his enemy. Make it clear what sign you wish and consider receiving the sign as guidance. You can even ask for answers to concrete questions as David does in I Samuel 23:10–12.

Let prayer for others, even for great sinners, be one of defense. Rabbi Nehemiah said, 'When the Israelites constructed and worshipped the golden calf, Moses sought to appease God's anger saying, "Lord of the universe, they have made an assistant for you. Why should You be angry with them? This calf will assist You: You will cause the sun to shine and the calf will cause the moon to shine; You will take care of the stars and the calf will take care of the planets; You will cause the dew to fall and the calf will make the winds to blow; You will cause the rain to fall and the calf will cause vegetation to sprout." The Holy One, praused be He, said to Moses, 'You are making the same mistake that the people are making! This calf is not real!" Moses then replied, "If that is so, why should You be angry with Your children" (Exodus Rabbah)?

Let your words with God also be wise and convincing.

A man can pray in any decent bodily position. Those with high calling sometimes use what we would call advanced Yoga positions, like Elijah who put his face between his knees, which is possible only after much physical exercise (I Kings 18:42).

Use your eyes in prayer. I do not know how the custom of closing the eyes in prayer arose. Jesus' habit was to lift them. The bridegroom in Solomon's song says to his bride, 'Thou has ravished my heart with one of thine eyes' (4:9). ('Having ravished the heart' is expressed by the single Hebrew word *levavtini*, which is the strongest word for uniting two hearts.)

Jesus is attentive to our eyes while we pray. He observed that a publican 'would not lift up so much as his eyes unto heaven,' knowing his own sinfulness, and says, 'this man went down to his house justified' (Luke 18:13–14).

At other times, believers show God great love through the expression in their eyes. Learn to use your eyes correctly in your communion with God and with men.

The author welcomes correspondence at this address:
   Christian Mission to the Communist World
      POB 19
      Bromley
      Kent BR1 1DY
      Britain